Men Explained, Finally

Tom Sturges

Cover Creative Direction & Design: Brian Hunt

Contents

PART 2

Men Compared to Women

PART 3

Men and Women Getting Together

Preface
by Dr. Mark P. Goodman, M.D.

Here you hold a serious yet humorous, approachable guide to men written by an accomplished gentleman who has long considered how to best describe men, and who has written other successful books on a variety of related subjects, notably including one about the man that was his dad.

Raised by a masterful screenwriter-director, Tom has not only had a prolific music executive career but is also a devoted husband, father, friend, author, educator, and public speaker. Beginning with *Parking Lot Rules & 75 Other Ideas for Raising Amazing Children*, and moving on to other titles including *Every Idea Is A Good Idea: Be Creative Anytime, Anywhere*, he last published *A Good Divorce Begins Here: A Guide to Surviving and Thriving Afterward*. His writing has been included in *Best Life* magazine, CNN, *People*, and *The New York Times*.

I have known Tom a number of years as a friend and the physician for him and two generations of his family from both marriages. A remarkably kind-spirited husband and father he has a generous heart, and a good understanding of people as he shepherded many through music careers. As children can reflect their parents' upbringing, you will not meet more kind, considerate or accomplished children as he has, and if character is revealed through both cooperation and conflict, his sweet current marriage and his amicable and enduring relationship with his previous spouse, he is a pillar for all who know him.

I have practiced internal medicine for 30 years. After my high school valedictorian address, I attended UCLA on each of the major available scholarships for academic and personal accomplishment, finishing with Departmental Honors in Biology. After medical school and residency there in Internal Medicine, I became a UCLA School of Medicine Assistant Clinical Professor of Medicine, and sat for many years on their Ethics Committee, and for a time on their medical school admissions committee. I helped develop curriculum for the socialization of a physician, and—as much as one can—teaching the humanistic care of how to relate sincerely and empathically to people, obviously including the men Tom describes here.

Being the multi-generational family physician that I've been for Tom and others involves both the art and science of medicine. Physicians obviously daily rely on the science and as such seek through research and study to obtain the most well established approach to preserving wellness and addressing illness; or incorporating the most reasoned progressive solution to extending life and happiness. The art of medicine however is every bit or more important than the science. It is through that that you connect with, and truly care for, people. And it is by understanding people that I can be an acceptable physician just as readily to someone that exercises daily and eats well as to the person that starts drinking at noon, but will only work with a physician that comprehends his limitations and can best incorporate that certain lifestyle into their care. So just as I care for the men in Tom's family, I have cared for women and lots of other men for decades, being there for wellness and sickness, cancer diagnoses and treatment, births and deaths, weddings and divorces, and dating. Of course I am one of them too, yet understanding men is important and it is something I practice every day.

Tom writes here his experience in accessible ways, often by analogies easily understood such as the similarity between "men and whales." His notion that dealing with men requires relating to a fourteen-year-old touches on the formative and important processes that occur at that time in the male maturity. And yet he writes about them in a manner more comprehensive than just sex. As he sees it, he incorporates their more deep feelings and thoughts, what his experience has shown him guides them as they tackle the "fate and luck" that he relates are instrumental in their lives. Perhaps Tom's secret to life has been in the practice of his "three rules," and if that is the trick, they are here for you to see.

For years, I have incorporated humor into my practice. And for some time, if I didn't tell a joke at a patient's visit, they would worry that there was something wrong with me, or them—and didn't know which scared them more. So Tom's incorporation here of humor is meaningful in making it more human. He writes in a heartwarming manner about the "mancharade" that he sees in how men act, and instills anecdotes throughout making this a pleasurable read.

My dad taught me it is not always only the very best that one seeks, but what is best for one individually. Tom's guide here helps one navigate that maze for men. His recounting of one way to understand the quality of the gentleman by how he treats his mom and a waiter is a point well made. Tom's chapter on "Have you seen my husband?" is an engaging discourse on how to approach a stranger. And to help you know if he is the one, Tom has his "seven questions." About whether you might be the one to change the man, reading Tom's section on "men are like great books" is enlightening. And while my own dad also thought about "too soon old, and too late smart"—through Tom's candid recounting of his experiences and stories, Tom shares his perception of how to help fix that for his readers here as they engage with men.

Whether one agrees with each concept or sees it just as Tom does doesn't take from the charm and insight he shares in a straightforward fashion from his successful personal experience. I imagine each reader will gain something different, but each something of value in navigating the maze of men that is life. Enjoy.

Introduction

Think how many men there are in the world. Fathers, sons, husbands, boyfriends, uncles, doctors, lawyers, pool boys and truck drivers. In addition to waiters, professors, shop clerks, construction workers, whomever and whatever. The list goes on and on. Men are everywhere, like flowers in parks and cracks in sidewalks. I'm no expert but I would say men are probably close to half of the world's population.

And a lot of people find men to be childish, immature, infantile, and often unwilling to make the slightest effort to grow up, ever. Yeah, so…?

Maybe that's one of our superpowers. Bluffing, that is. We like to act like we know what we're doing, no matter what is happening and especially if we *don't* know what we're doing. We love to take charge! Fire first and ask all those silly questions later. Fib and filibuster and pretend we are right until it's so completely obvious that we're *not* right that we finally *have to* accept what has happened. And then we try to blame it on someone else anyway. It's been working so well, for so long, why change now?

This book arrives as a byproduct of my discoveries of a whole lot of man truths. And while I may be rebuked by some of the fellas for having written and revealed what I have written and revealed, none of them will disagree with the basic premise or foundational promise of this work. I would bet many of them don't even know this stuff about themselves, even though they enjoy the privileges of it every day.

TS/Los Angeles

PART 1

Men

Regardless of where or when you might run into one, men are similar. I'm not denying all the differences, just saying that men are much more like other men than they would probably like to admit. For instance...

Men Are Fourteen, Forever

A lot of men reach a moment early in their lives when they come to the realization that they are pretty much as developed as they will ever need to be. This is usually right around fourteen, or thereabouts. Some of us are very serious young men at this moment whose road in life is paved and smooth. Others are still bubbling in a chaotic soup of immaturity and there is no clear path ahead at all. But whatever the case, when we arrive at this age, we all start to arrive at the same conclusion, mainly that this much maturity is more than enough.

It's not lazy. It's just practical. Saves us a lot of time. The guy we are at this stage is likely to be the guy we are going to be from now on.

Whether that is a good man or a bad man, a thoughtful one or a thoughtless one, a giver or a taker, a thief or a priest, straight or gay, the pieces are all in place. Life has begun. Officially. This is who we are. The line has been crossed, the cement has been poured. The dice are rolling down the table.

Being fourteen, we now start to make our own first independent choices. Critical choices. Choices that will guide us for the rest of our lives, most likely. We decide what we are going to love about life, whether food or music or art or architecture. We decide what beauty is and chase a version of it literally for the rest of our lives. We decide what sports we are going to be fans of, and how manic we are willing to be about it. We decide what foods we like to eat and which ones we will never even try. We decide on the things that will terrify us the rest of the way, whether spiders or snakes or dark rooms or ghosts, and allow ourselves to be terrorized by them for always. Whether we want to or not, we decide our biases and prejudices, and right or wrong, we will stick with them until we're old guys. For many of us, religion is a choice that gets made in this critical period too, though often this one is hammered into place by our culture or our parents.

Once these foundational decisions get made, well then, let the games begin. And to a fourteen-year-old boy life is a game to be played.

We pretend until we're discovered. We fib until we fail. We fake it 'til we make it. We shoulder on until we get found out. You see the 14-year-old boy in us in almost everything we do. Even scared to death, we are still full of bravado. Even when being questioned for doing something very questionable, we deny it, at least first and foremost. Even if we are caught with our hand in a cookie jar, we will probably insist that our hand was *supposed* to be in the cookie jar, and we might even say it was part of our plan to see who's been stealing the cookies. We are proudly bluffing our way through almost everything we try to do, hoping we appear to be someone we're not, and believing that somehow we are pulling it off. We live most of our lives like underage kids with a phony ID trying to buy beer at the liquor store.

Along the way, we have learned that when in doubt, pretend to know. That makes things so much simpler. We just keep up the myth until we find the time to actually research whatever it is we say we're experts in, which we never will. We learn to say "Uh-huh" just enough times to keep the rest of you in doubt. Our undying belief in ourselves and our ability to keep pulling off the grand charade again and again is a big part of a simple philosophy that guides most of our lives: We know we have to get older but we also know we never have to grow up.

We are not trapped by being fourteen forever. It's not a prison. Not at all. It's our passport to get the most out of every day we're alive. It's our permission slip to get in and out of as much trouble and intrigue as we can possibly find ourselves getting in and out of. Honestly, it's our dream come true before we even know we have a dream. The whole idea of being fourteen forever is as central to our lives as central can possibly get, like a circular staircase in a lighthouse. Call it "Peter Pan Syndrome" or "Immaturity" or "Failure to Launch." Or call it whatever you like. We honestly don't care all that much what anyone calls it. We're living it.

For us, fourteen years old isn't a choice. It's a ride.

What Most Men and Whales Have in Common

One of the key reliable identifiers of a whale is the many scars and cuts and grooves on its back and fluke (aka its tail fin). Whales get hit by boats and propellers. Shot at by harpoons. They get bitten by sharks. They run into debris. And every encounter leaves its mark. The whale's skin heals but the scars remain for its entire lifetime.

Men get bumped and bruised and cut and scraped throughout their lifetimes too. We find ourselves in bad situations that we should not have been in. We find ourselves hanging out with people we should not have been hanging out with. We find ourselves alone when we should not be alone. And so it goes, throughout our adolescence and early years and later years. Throughout *all* our years. Some call it a Rite of Passage. Others just call it life. The scars left by these steps and missteps are not necessarily physical and not easy to see. Often, they are hidden and we never know what will bring them to light. Just like the whale cannot see the gouges and troughs in its back left by the screws of the oil tankers and fishing boats, men cannot see their scars either. But we know they are there. Seen or unseen, the scars are the proof that a man paid the price to survive and get that far in his life.

My friend Mike was sixteen years old when his car got broadsided driving down Sunset Boulevard, breaking his femur, tibia and hip and one of his arms and instantly ending his very promising athletic career. He got into that car as one of the hottest quarterback prospects in the South Bay and got out of it with completely different prospects. During his senior year he watched the kid who he had bested for years lead *his* team to the city championship. The team that he should have led. He's still getting over it. He builds houses now but looks like a boy who just lost a kitten. Another friend, Gene, was the only Jewish kid in our Catholic school. He got tossed into the dumpster most afternoons for years by the older boys. He trains UFC fighters now. Nobody gets over him or gets the best of him, and that has been the case for decades. He learned the hard way that his fists were his best friends.

Whether it was bad luck, or bad circumstances, or being in the wrong place at the wrong time, our lives are often marked by the scars left behind by these kinds of encounters. For most men there is some event that upended their lives and sent them off into a completely unintended or unexpected direction. Might have been a bad coach, or an unfair punishment for an unimportant minor offense. My pal Mark's son was kicked off his baseball team for answering a question honestly about whether he went to a party where beer was served to minors. The coach wanted to set an example, so he cut Mark's son off the team and in so doing cut Mark's son's life in half. All these years later, the boy (now a man) still can't believe it.

For others of us, it might have been an early romance that went off the rails for no good reason, never giving an explanation that made any sense. Or we just made a bad choice and ended up in the very wrong place at the very wrong time. Or it was bad luck, and there's always plenty of that when you're growing up. Though we survived, somehow, it was not without a cost. Our innocence was, from then on, much less innocent. Our naiveté was distorted. We experienced a diminishment of our dreams, a loss of our hopes. We got humbled by life and its difficult choices. Whether having been preyed upon by a con artist and their tricks, or having been scammed by some liar, every single one of us goes through something. Way too much of the time, the damage is self-inflicted – usually by drugs or alcohol – changing the arc of any boy's life. And the marks are forever.

But we keep going. We keep trying to make right those things that life made wrong, where we learned the hard way. We know things are going to get better at some point. They just have to...

Every man knows he is far from perfect. He knows he has lost some of himself along the way, that he is missing some things, that there are imperfections all over him... But there he is, shouldering on, hoping that his luck will maybe, just maybe, change at last.

At the end of the day, if he is going to survive and live a life worth living, a man must believe in a better future. He must be an optimist. He just has to. Without his optimism, he's got nothing. So, he compartmentalizes away the outrageous and unfair, the unkindness and the heartbreak. He entertains the dream that things are going to turn around, any minute now. He moves forward hoping that what has been an empty space, like his heart, maybe, will soon be filled and fulfilled. He dreams that what has been stripped and torn away, maybe his ability to believe in the impossible, will be replaced and even reborn somehow. He hopes that those things that have been taken from him unfairly, like his innocence, will return somehow. He fantasizes that what has been lost forever, like his kid dreams, will be found somehow.

Whales keep swimming, no matter what. Men keep living, no matter what.

Seeds of Manhood Get Planted Early

I was getting one of my sons dressed for school one day and, as usual, I let him choose his own clothes. He was seven. That particular day was Teacher Appreciation Day. All the students had been asked to wear something turquoise to honor the staff.

The one and only turquoise shirt my boy owned was a disaster. Maybe because it came out of the dirty laundry hamper. It smelled strongly of socks. Portions of the previous day's lunch stretched down the front in fine brown streaks. Plus there was grass and mud from the park and the business end of a gummy bear stared out from a fold.

I said, "Son, that shirt... is *really* dirty. You might even be embarrassing yourself if you wear it..." He looked up at me. "I know, Dad. But it's okay. We're men." Yikes.

Ask Nicely – A Man Will Do Almost Anything

Men aim to please. Well, we want to aim to please. Most of the time anyway. We love pleasing. We are, givers, by and large. Yes there are some notable exceptions of course, but generally speaking we do what has to be done and take care of whatever it is that needs to be taken care of.

Possibly this trait has its origins when we were cavemen armed only with sharp sticks. I see us through the grainy mists of time, realizing that if we didn't clean out the cave or hunt down the occasional wooly mammoth, that no one else was going to do it. We must have understood that it was also up to us to keep the fire going and gather beans and berries and draw on the walls. Gradually over the years this responsibility morphed into a key element of our manhood (or should we just call it what it really is: our boyhood) and has stayed with us, right here into the present day. So here we are. Ready to go. Willing. Able. Available to do things for the rest of you in the cave with us.

But, as with anything, there's a catch. But you probably knew that anyway if you have ever spent any time with one of us. We have to be asked nicely. It's a must. A request cannot sound like an order, or a demand. Or worse, like some kind of command. We have to be made to feel like we are the only person in the world who could do this particular thing that needs doing, even if it's running to the drugstore for a prescription or untying a knotted up shoelace. As a ridiculous example, in *The Godfather*, Bonasera the mortician insulted Don Corleone because he didn't ask him in just the right way to break someone's legs. Okay, same thing here but without the broken legs.

If it's something only we can do and you ask us in the right way, the job is practically finished before it's begun. My wife has this down to a science, maybe because she's become a Husband Whisperer. She'll say, "My Tom? Could I ask you a huge favor…?" And that's it. I'm in. I'm saying yes before she even finishes making the request. I always answer in the affirmative and yes I always will. It almost doesn't matter what the request is at that point. Just the way she asks makes me feel like I'm the only guy within miles capable of doing whatever it is that needs doing.

Men Still Have Their Forts

When we were little boys, one of the great discoveries we made was the concept of the fort. Our private sanctuary. Our secret spot. Even though it was right in the middle of the living room, and only made out of blankets and pillows. Nonetheless we came to believe that no one could see us, no one could know what we were doing and no one would ever dare to bother us. As long as we were in our fort, the world was far away. It was our very own private Garden of Eden. But no Eve, no apples, no snakes. There in our moment of paradise no one could disturb us. The fort was our protection and part of our little boy myth. I have fathered, lived with and helped raise three little boys, so far. Starting at three or four years old or or so, each one of them had a fort up in the family room that was ready to protect them long before I awoke. It was most often a ratty old Afghan stretched between a sofa and an easy chair, but it might as well have been the Pentagon.

Cut ahead a few years in every man's life and the fort mentality continues. We don't call it a fort anymore, though most of us still have one. Now we call it a man cave, a wine cellar, a music room, a studio or a home office. In some cases, we maybe just call it what it is: the garage. If we are on top of the world at this point, like a CEO or the owner of some amazing company, our office has become the fort. We have our own private bathroom, and triple locking doors have replaced the stacks of toys that used to defend the perimeter. My good friend Bob lives in a nice place up on a hill overlooking a city. And his whole house is basically his fort. There's a pool table in the dining room, an air hockey table in the den, a bar shuffleboard in the breakfast area, big screen televisions on several walls, and the two refrigerators are stuffed with beer and frozen pizza. The guest bathroom even has a potty putter! Talk about the perfect fort, I mean, c'mon!

Whatever they are, or wherever they might be, there, in our forts, we are safe. We are alone. We are invisible. We can be totally ourselves, at least for a few minutes. We can scratch ourselves, hoist a few petards, click on anything we want to see on the internet and not offend any of the other adults in the area. While in our forts we are experts at everything and failures at nothing. In our forts we are, and always will be, invincible. Regardless of how it relates to our maturity, or lack of it, a fort is often a key element of how we survived the first part of our lives, our childhood. It is also a buffer that helps us survive this, the much longer lasting and much more complicated part of our lives.

Men Love Forever

Ask the guy nearest you if he remembers the first girl he ever fell in love with. Odds are he can tell you her first and last name and still has a couple of stories about their first look or first kiss, or how things never actually got that far. He can undoubtedly remember her hair or her smell or the way she got into her mom's car after school because this first romance most likely took place in the fourth or fifth grade. Or he remembers some clever thing she said once ten thousand days ago. Why does a man still remember? Because her impact on him and his heart was great and grand and *for always*. It's like when all those meteors strike the moon and leave behind all those craters. It's still the moon, it's just got a bunch of craters on it. A man's heart is still his heart, it's just got a bunch of dents from all the 'fall in loves' he experienced.

But it's not just a mark from the first girl. There's the girl in seventh grade, and the one in high school, and maybe one in college. There is the first adult romance, and the second, and whatever else happened on his way to meet the person he was supposed to meet all along. Like a clear path through a beautiful garden, all those interludes gave him a route to follow until he found the latest, and hopefully greatest love of his life.

If he was in love with someone, whether it was a real relationship, or a fling, or just some beauty on the subway, whoever they were, the memory of those loves will never go away. Sure they'll fade, but they'll never die. A man does not do this because he wants to, it just happens. It's an *is*. It's the boy never forgetting the perfection of an emotion that was so fresh and new to him, and so thrilling, and so everything, once upon a time long ago.

This is not to say that he still wants to be pals with all the women he ever loved. When it comes to old loves, men much prefer their memories to their realities. Knowing past loves has little or nothing to do with present day happiness. If we happen to bump into someone at a high school reunion or a department store, it's all very friendly, but trying to re-ignite the old flame is pure idiocy. We read that book. We saw that movie. We know all the secrets waiting to be revealed. To see an old love now, especially in some romantic way, would destroy the perfect image of who she *was*, what she was, and what she meant to him when she was the girl from way back when. There is a reason we call it "Glory Days."

Men are infatuated with their own innocence, and what it meant to them, and how it felt as little bits and pieces of that innocence chipped away. And as every new love affair came and went, more and more innocence disappeared. Meanwhile the heart gets stronger and better at loving.

By the time we are all grown up, or allegedly all grown up anyway, men know that those early love affairs were just that: early love affairs. They are wisps of memories that cannot really compare to the beautiful reality of the later loves that eclipsed them. When he happens to think of an old girlfriend, maybe because he heard the song that mattered back then, or was reminded of a film they saw together, he will remember a girl from long ago and he will touch the mark on his heart, tracing what's left of the scar she left behind. And for the briefest of moments, relive the beauty of what once was.

As an example, when my mom was still alive and well into her seventies, and cell phones were not as ubiquitous as they are today, she would get a call almost every Saturday morning. It was from a payphone somewhere in Pittsburgh, PA. (For those of you who have no idea what I'm talking about, once upon a time a phone call required pumping pocket change into a steel box and shouting over the street noise outside the booth you were standing in. Primitive times…)

On the other end of the line was a man named Tommy, who was just another boy who loved her when they were both in high school. He went off to fight WWII and she went off and married Ralph, the next guy who asked her to a dance. She barely remembered Tommy when he came home from D-Day, by then a veteran who had aged a decade in the year he was away. Yet he never ever forgot her. Almost sixty years had gone by and still he filled his pockets with quarters and dimes and hustled down to the drugstore near his house to call my mom and share a few stories and a few laughs about their old days. He was the father of many children and the grandfather of many more by this time. He didn't want to see my mom, or date her, or anything like that. His calls weren't romantic in any way. He just wanted to *talk* to her. He just wanted to remember. To relive. To remember her and to be sure that she still remembered him. He was never able to let go of the overwhelming feelings he had for her, the girl he fell for when he was just a kid getting shipped off to fight in a war. Until the day he passed away, he always loved my mom, the first girl he ever loved.

Why? Because in some way or another, men will love every girl they ever loved, no matter how long ago it was, forever.

Those earlier love affairs, whether they hap-pened when we were 6, 16, 36, or 60, are the stepping stones that guide us to today. Without those experiences to rely upon, and all the smiles and heartbreaks that remain intact in our memories, we would not be able to find happiness in the here and now, as alleged grownups. We would not be able to give in to the present, or to allow ourselves to fall in love just one more time, had we not learned how to survive giving in to love earlier. Had we not had our hearts broken then, we could not love now.

If we're lucky, and many of us are, sooner or later we do meet the woman we're supposed to meet, the woman we are supposed to spend the rest of our days with, the one we were meant to know all along. The last love can be the greatest love, regardless of how many great loves came before it.

Our First Line of Defense: Compartmentalize

Compartmentalization is a protection mechanism. We all do it. Not because we choose to, but because we have to. We turn our individual life into hundreds of separate little lives, and deal with things as close as possible to one at a time. This is key to our survival. It's the only way the boy in us can deal with all the crazy, grown up, *adult* things coming at us.

Long ago we must have discovered that compartmentalizing was the only way to endure the entire adventure without losing our minds and somehow passed the skill of how to do it along to all the other men. Like some kind of species shifting, intergenerational version of murmuration. And now, all of us dudes survive using the same basic system. We know that each and every one of our many component lives has its own compartments into which we put all the things about it that matter, and if we don't want to deal with what's in there, we just close the box and move on.

Think about it. We are so many people all wrapped up into one guy… And every single "thing" about us has its own box.

There is no limit to the number of boxes we have, and there are always more where those came from anyway. We can use fifty in a day, or five, it just depends on how crazy that day is going. There are boxes for everything we have to do and deal with, everyone and everything we know and knew, and all the events we have already lived through and would like to forget. The walls of these boxes are usually very thick, and thus the emotions and problems from one box rarely leak into another.

A man can have a daylong dispute with a co-worker and then have a great time with him/her/them at a poker game or a bowling alley that evening. How? No problem. Two separate boxes. Another man might have a noisy argument with his wife and then be ready to start a perv-party with her just a few minutes after the argument is over. Easy. Two different boxes. Get out of the one and get into the other. How else can a fourteen-year-old juggle all the competing interests and desires, people and places, inexplicable embarrassments and undeniable truths life throws at him? There is only one defense that handles this kind of traffic: Compartmentalization! Whatever it is, we just put it in a box! Emotions, complications, a tax lien, the overdue rent… He who can compartmentalize best can survive almost anything.

Men are able to leave behind the messes they've made, and the boxes they are in, and embrace the good times, and the boxes they are in, without the slightest hesitation. We hop from box to box like a kangaroo jumping from shrub to shrub. This skill is key to our sense of self, and our self-protection.

Regardless of what disaster may have just befallen, there is always a box to put it in, and another one nearby that is easy enough to step into and hide and forget for a while. Bad day at school? Put it in the box and play some video games. Bad day at work? Put it in the box and find a watering hole, quick! Bad day all around? Put it in the box and just fuhgeddaboudit!!!

Can you imagine if we had no boxes? If all our issues and problems were just out there, spread all around? Every mistake and embarrassment on display, forever? Men would never survive. If we don't have a place to hide the bad, we'll never be able to find a way to see the good.

While there are many positives in our compartment system, there are some downsides too. Sometimes a man is in a box by choice, and sometimes he has no choice at all. Revenge, regret, envy and jealousy are four compartments that compromise a lot of men's lives. These boxes are huge.

And close to each other too. Like crack houses. It's wwwwway too easy to step out of one and right into another. And if he's not careful, there are circumstances where a man can get stuck in one bad box and get completely lost in it. He simply cannot find an exit. He might not come out for weeks or months, years even. Think about all the psychos out there that are truly stuck in some very bad boxes that they will never open. Bottoms like quicksand.

We men survive as well as we do because we compartmentalize the way we do, with our thoughts and dreams and emotions all carefully tucked away in a semi-well-organized system that almost works. Our *Fears and Failures* box is stored away and hard to find. Our *Stupid Things I Said* box is hopefully high on a shelf in the back. Our *Heroic Acts & Good Deeds* box is always close at hand in case we need to remind someone what a remarkable person we are.

So, here's the point, and the reason why I share this facet of men and their survival. If the man that matters to you most disappears into a box, know that it has less to do with him than you might think. Maybe he's lost and is simply trying to find himself again. Maybe he was reminded of something he did that he wished he didn't do, and he's down in a box trying to figure out why he did that thing in the first place. Who really knows and who will ever know but the man himself...?

We compartmentalize as a defense mechanism. A defense against the complications of the life we are living, and the sorrow of the dreams we did not achieve. Because no matter how hard we try we can never forget the promises we forgot to keep. Or the injustice we've known. Sad memories fly around our hearts like bees around a hive, darting in and out. It's just the way it is. And the only way to defend against the sting is to wrap that memory up tight and hide it away. At least for a little while.

So if a man has gotten lost in one of his boxes, be patient. Let him find himself again, on his time-line, not yours. Let him compartmentalize. It's one of the things men do so well.

Most Rich Men Have
a Poor Friend

This is one of the craziest things about us and I can't explain the how or the why or the wherefor, but it's a thing. Rich man, poor friend.

Maybe it reminds them of their days when they were broke too? Had nothing and no responsibilities. Before marriages and children and all the rest. Maybe it gives them one person they can be completely themselves around. Someone who knew them when. Or maybe it's just proof that things actually do get lonely at the top.

My very wealthy friend Chris, who is a wonderful man and a very good friend even all these years later, had his hangeron. Or is that Hanger-On...? His pal Des would join us for dinner or drinks, and was always too happy, and too delighted to be there, and too obsequious to be believed. But there he was. Every time Chris came to town, Des joined us. In his old suit and his tired eyes. He told us a brilliant story every time we met. (In one of them he was lost on an island near Sweden when the guide for his boy scout troupe fell into a crevasse and died. Along with the walkie talkie and maps…)

They were equals of a sort, because Des knew Chris when Chris was just beginning. Chris turned out to be a genius at music and songs and producing and so forth, and Des turned out to be an okay waiter. And there's the fork in the road. But each of them reminded each other of the past – when things were much simpler.

I had the privilege of working for Shaq. I ran his label and organized a tour of the Far East we called "Shaq's Rap & Jam." He loved all his "First Days," a term assigned to pals who were there at the beginning. He gave them gigs and a reason to stick around, lots of opportunities to keep them in his universe. They were all broke, and basically poor, at least compared to him. And it was not lost on me that he always wanted them around. They were his pals. They reminded him of his youth and his innocence. They grounded him. Maybe that's all they had to offer, and maybe that's all he wanted.

Rich men, poor friends.

Men and Sex

Let's make this simple. There's never enough.

Sex is something we think about whenever there's nothing else to think about, or even when there is something else to think about. Doesn't matter.

Its attraction never goes away, and it's never *not* on a list of things to do that day. And it's usually the best part of whatever day it happens to happen on.

The only other thing you can say that about is carrot cake.

A Lot of Men Think They Can Do Anything

Men have an impossibly grand belief that anything is possible. If we just put enough time and effort into almost any thought, we can make it a reality. This is a trait that is key to our lives, our whereabouts, and the achievements of our collective destiny. We are who we are because men believed that there was nothing they could not do, nothing that could not be done. This foundational element of mankind can be seen in every aspect of our history: all the explorers, dreamers, artists, inventors. We truly have them to thank. And, it must be said, to blame.

Everyone who starts a business from scratch is one of these dreamers. Everyone who asks the love of his life to get married and have some kids is one of them. Anyone who tries to build their own house or run their own farm is one of them. Every man who gets up in the morning without a job and goes to stand in some line hoping to get one, is one of them. Just to survive men have to believe in themselves and their ability to pull off anything and everything that comes to mind. Legal, illegal, brand new or as old as dirt. Tried and true or spur of the moment. Huge idea or tiny one.

Men are gifted with the ability to have faith in the impossible and try to make it all work somehow. Some of these fantasies come to be, and the results are remarkable and everlasting. But some of us never learn. Or only learn the hard way. This beautiful instinct to believe that anything is possible has also found its way into men's less than admirable behavior. The same belief that helps us conquer the planet and build skyscrapers and travel to Mars is also being used by every cheat and swindler out there. Document forgers, jewel thieves, tax-evaders, bank robbers, Bitcoin heisters and criminals of all sizes and descriptions borrow from our brave ancestors with every con they try. But their idiocy doesn't make the trait any less noble or admirable.

So should it be the case that a man you love wants to try something almost impossible or seemingly ridiculous, who knows, why not try it? He's just following in the footsteps of all the big dreamers who came before him and he might be on to something great.

A Few Are Just Marauders

A marauder is someone who sees something and decides that it should be theirs, regardless of who already owns that thing. Comes from the French word for "rascal" but it's more like a drunk rascal on fentanyl laced cocaine. Marauders look at the world as though it already belongs to them and the only question remaining is when they will take complete ownership of it. No one and nothing means more than their own contentment and the satisfaction of their own acquisitive desires. They don't want to know what anyone else knows, because they think they know all they need to know. They believe whatever they think is truth, whatever they dream up is fact, and whatever they want should be theirs. It's like they live in a snow globe and cannot see past the glass.

The planet's earliest land explorers were marauders. As were all the real pirates of the Caribbean (circa 1500-1750). Slavers were marauders, who changed the world with their evil. And every single one of the despots and dictators you can name are in the fraternity too. One would have hoped that their miserable traits would have disappeared through some kind of natural selection but sadly that is not the case. There are just as many out there today as there were in all the years before. Marauders are rife with 14 year old boy traits and characteristics, but it's as if they've been sprinkled with some kind of pixie dust that doubles and triples the least desirable of their natures. Marauders are us 14 year old boys at our absolute worst.

Sadly, very sadly, and I'm not exactly sure how, marauders often end up in charge. Of the schoolyard. Of the gang. Of companies. Of countries. They wrap themselves in the language of peace and wage wars. They cover their lies with hints of expertise and hope no one notices it's all a grand deceit. Marauders attack with sudden violence and catch their unsuspecting enemies, or citizens in many cases, completely off guard. They like to accuse their challengers of doing exactly what they themselves are actually doing.

Hitler was a marauder. Probably the worst of the worst. There were several other powerful morons who aligned themselves with his practices and did the same to their people around the same time. Mussolini, Franco, Stalin, Tojo. Then later, Peron, Pinochet, Mao Zedong, Duvalier, Samozo and Kim Il Sung. They learned from the best and wiped millions of people off the face of the earth in service to their insanity. Almost every war has begun with a marauder who wanted more than he already had and didn't really care all that much how he went about getting it.

Power corrupts and absolute power corrupts absolutely. Marauders could care less about how corrupted they become because if they are powerful enough, no one can do anything about it anyway. In the present day, we have many. Putin is one. Maduro is another. And there are plenty more. Put the word "Dictator" into a search engine and over fifty names come up. All of them have much in common, but first on the list of commonalities is that they see the world only through their own lens, and make decisions based only on what would be best for them.

Marauders are the boys who completely lost their way. They try to make all the rest of us look bad. Like those Purple Minions in Despicable Me 2.

Not sure if you noticed but there are no female marauders.

Men and Heroism

Heroes are what most men hope to be. One way or another.

Many of us are brave, fearless, and dedicated believers in things and ideas much bigger and much grander than ourselves. Many of us are willing to risk our lives every day so that the rest of the population doesn't have to. Men at their best, men at their finest. Sailors. Soldiers. Fireman. Police. Secret Service. First Responders. Second Responders. Doctors. Nurses. Etc.

But not all of us are *that* kind of hero. Many of us are heroes in other ways. Maybe not doing things quite as dangerous as putting out fires or dropping pallets of food into starving nations, but still doing things that require a lot of bravery. How about taking the family camping? Or cleaning out the rain gutters? Or losing a little weight? No, not as dangerous as an ambulance driver, but it's quite a battle to undertake regardless.

How about driving an older dog to the vet in the middle of the night? Or racing across town to rescue a frightened nine-year old from a lousy sleepover? Or taking an ex-mother-in-law car shopping? Or coaching 25 youth soccer teams? No, that is not like getting shot at by some lunatic in a faraway place but it's still heroism. Of a sort.

Just like a dog is a descendant of the mighty wolf, a man of today is a descendant of some mighty men from long ago. Somewhere in every one of our family trees there were prototype alpha males who heroically did heroic things. Conquerors, Explorers, Artists, Architects, Astronauts, Builders too. Heroes come in many shapes and sizes, in degrees of heroism, and in ways you might not always expect. Some are grand achievements that save nations and some are smaller achievements that save little boys' broken hearts.

A lot of men are heroes in one way or another, doing good deeds and making the world a better and safer place to live. And we all have something in common, us heroic types. We do things *not* just for the benefit of ourselves but for the benefit of others.

Please try to remember this next time we forget your birthday.

Genius, Idiot or Both

Men can often do one or two things really well. And I mean really well. Splitting atoms. Sending rockets into space. Performing open heart surgery. That kind of thing. But often, in other things they try, the result is chaos. This is true regardless of social standing, education, country or county of origin, religious beliefs, whatever. Brilliant executives are often distant and disconnected parents. Artists and actors are stars to the world but rarely as nice in private as they appear to the public. Authors and poets build words and phrases into monuments that last for decades yet many of them can barely carry on a normal conversation. Many men, inside their area of expertise, are unmatched. But when they step outside the circle of their great genius, almost anything can happen. Albert Einstein figured out how the universe was put together but couldn't keep his marriage from falling apart – he wrote notes to his wife that he would leave around the house telling her to please leave him alone. My auntie was married for many years to the acclaimed author Malcolm Lowry.

He could create lasting and truly extraordinary works of fiction (*Under The Volcano* for instance) and cook chicken gumbo like a New Orleans native but he couldn't tie his shoes or stay sober for longer than two days in a row. Like most of us guys, it seems, he could do one or two things brilliantly but kept lousing up everything else.

As an example of man at his most idiot-savant, there is one I knew. He will have to go unnamed, and when you read what he did, or at least tried to do until I stopped him, you will see why I will be keeping his name out of the public circus. He was an impossible genius and an impossibly jealous adolescent, all in one person. Like a lot of us.

He had been awarded two PhD's from two of the most prestigious institutions of higher learning in the civilized world. His books on how to remove certain kinds of cancer in certain parts of the body are still considered the finest written on the subject and are both textbooks used in a significant percentage of medical schools in the world. He was accorded with the respect he deserved in every gathering of his peers and was awarded medals of accomplishment from his native government on several occasions. He was treasured by all who knew him, and everyone whose life he saved.

But slip outside his penumbra of unmatched brilliance, and he was an anxious doubtful 14-year-old boy who overflowed with terrible ideas. He tried very hard to involve me in one of his worst ones (at least I *hope* it was his worst!). It started when his girlfriend was visiting New York to work on a film project that had been close to her heart for years and years. She finally found a few other believers, including a film producer neither of them really knew. But the only place the girlfriend could stay that made any economic sense for the two months the project would take was at the producer's house, there overlooking a park.

Once the project was underway, during one phone call or another, 2PhD's heard a note in his girlfriend's voice that sounded strangely different and distant, and on top of which she did not say "I love you..." in the melody he had grown used to. 2PhD's immediately did what many men would do in that situation. He panicked. He decided that she was probably sleeping with the producer, and that this was probably the reason she went there in the first place, and that all was probably lost, and that short of killing himself, his next best option was to catch her in the act. That way at least he could protect his broken heart and whatever shreds and shards might be left of his dignity. This was based on absolutely *nothing*. He had imagined the whole thing.

Something idiotic boys will often do.

But before he came to his senses, he came up with an idea. A terrible idea. An idea that only a jealous fool would think was a good idea. Or should I say it was an idea most fourteen-year-old year-old boys would think was absolutely perfect in all respects. *His idea was for me to break into the producer's house!* And once inside, to plant a recording device in the guest bedroom where the girlfriend was staying. It was a recording device that was voice activated, so that the necessary evidence could be gathered to prove 2PhD's suspicions without needlessly using up the battery. (I guess it's always a good idea to save on battery expenses when plotting crimes…) He actually sent along the recorder, and also the security code to the alarm system, which 2PhD's had whee-dled out of his girlfriend a few days before. When I asked how the device would be retrieved, he replied that obviously the house would have to be broken into *a second time* so I could retrieve it. How bril-liant. And so obvious. Why hadn't I thought of that?

So, let's review. This genius, truly one of the smartest men in the world, was asking me to com-mit two felonies, two break-ins, just to see if his girl-friend was as faithful to him as she had promised she would be. Or to learn that she was shacking up with her host, who had done nothing but offer her a place to stay? My friend, 2PhD's, had gone to school for almost 15 years and was one of the most decorated men in his field and *that* was what he came up with? That was his solution? With no evidence of any sort of indiscretion on her part other than the way she said "Goodnight?"

He was, quite seriously, asking me to risk my life, my treasure, and my freedom, simply to prove the possibility of his impossible thesis, which only existed to support his infantile theory. He was doing all of this to confirm something that he wouldn't want confirmed anyhow. The fact that he was asking me to break several laws never occurred to him as a reason to find another solution. Or just come to his senses.

After a few weeks of his insanity and begging, I declined the chance to go to prison on his behalf. This wasn't easy. But I finally talked him off the ledge by reminding him that she was just not that kind of person and would no sooner mess around behind his back than she would kick their dog. I sent him back the recorder and never breathed a word about the whole thing to anybody. The girlfriend came home totally unaware of what had gone on while she was away. They got married, had two brilliant kids and touched the happily ever after button for several years. He never lost his mind like that again.

I will never forget the lesson the experience provided me, nor the wisdom (or the *lack* of wisdom) inherent in it. 2PhD's was the ultimate man. Successful. Accomplished. Admired, respected and rewarded. A man among men. Yet inside, still driven by childish jealousy, and full of painfully stupid ideas. In many respects he is a living breathing example of the kind of dilemmas many men face just getting up in the morning. On the one hand, genius. On the other hand, idiot.

Men really have little control over what's happening inside their heads. Almost none. Some days we are absolutely brilliant. Other days we are absolutely stupid. Most of the time, we are blissfully unaware which of these positions we might be in, while pretending to be great at everything and hoping no one is noticing that we are only good at a few things.

More than anything else, this completely ridiculous scenario speaks to the undeniable fact that inside every man is a fourteen-year-old boy. A boy who might be terribly immature on some days and surprisingly brilliant on other days. A boy who, even in the middle of a many years long relationship, can still have doubts that his partner is in fact faithful to him. A boy who can stray well beyond reason and common sense with hardly any reason at all. This also proves beyond any doubt, again, that no man really knows how or why the woman who loves him loves him.

So if you find yourself in a relationship with one of us, please strap on your safety belt and just enjoy the ride. He's in the driver's seat of his own life but I promise you he's barely even steering. So, what to do, what to do? Be patient and understanding. Limit your judgements until you hear the whole story. And should the chance arrive, just give him the benefit of the doubt.

There are storms of childish idiocy that rage inside every man right alongside his rivers of passion, his oceans of hope, his skies full of genius. He is in control of none of them. It's like men are watching the same movie the rest of you are, just sitting a little closer to the screen.

A Good Percentage of Men Don't Tell the Truth

Not all men are liars, but all of us know how to do it. When it comes to height, weight, career achievements, bank balances, how much we love our jobs, or hate them, how little we paid for the house, how much we paid for the car, how many watches, how many girls, how many anything… Probably all just grand exaggerations. Plenty of us are allergic to the truth, like any fourteen-year-old would be.

Some men don't lie about just the important things; they prevaricate about almost anything. Sometimes just to see if they can still get away with it. Sometimes just to see if the rest of you are even listening. And, of course, sometimes just for a laugh, like when someone farts in an elevator and the rest of us point at the guy in the dumb hat.

At the same time, some of us should maybe lie more. We share every detail of an experience, good bad or stupid. We discuss at length the minutiae of recent health news, or divulge our blood pressure issues to waiters. Frankly, not every story deserves to be told, but a lot of us fourteen year olds forget this and tell everyone everything, whether it's precisely accurate or not. I can only assume these fellas are operating under the terms of a famous Ralph Waldo Emerson theorem: "The truth is beautiful, but so are lies."

But there is a method to the madness, really... In so many ways, for most of us, every single day is a sham of one kind or another. We are pretending to be the men you see, the men you married, the men you trust with your secrets. We are pretending to be wise and all-knowing and completely in charge. But this scam only works if the rest of you fall in line and keep believing our version of the truth. Sometimes we keep the lie going because we cannot believe that the ruse is still working, and that we've pulled it off this well for this long. Sometimes we lie because we can't hardly believe that the rest of you people, the ones who actually love us, continue to love us! Honestly, and this is not a lie, we don't know why you do and we're afraid to ask.

Follow me on this. It makes no sense that all of you, our partners and lovers, are still our partners and lovers. And sometimes that confusion lasts forever. What are you people thinking?!@? You signed up for this...? We are children, after all, dressed up in grown men's clothes and nice shoes, with passports and such, pretending to be the husband and father you see us pretending to be, pretending to be the judges and the lawyers you see, pretending to be all the folks we are supposed to be. Okay, there it is. The whole thing is just a bluff!

We are dancing to music we can't even hear. We are playing a part in a play, but we've never read the script. This whole scenario that you might call life is a complete dream come true for us every single day. And we don't want anyone else to figure it out. We're faking it folks, and we can't believe the rest of you are still buying it. We just want to keep the truth about us hidden for a little while longer.

If you want to see a pack of lies, go to Indeed. com or LinkedIn and start looking at the resumes that are posted there. Ridiculous for the most part. Every other line is a complete exaggeration of responsibility and value to the companies named. Want to hear lies like you've never heard lies before? Go to a funeral and listen to what get said about the dearly departed. I attended one a few years ago that left me stupefied. The deceased was a liar, a cheat and a convicted thief, and I knew some of his victims. But there he was in the box, his few virtues getting extolled like he was the closest anyone had ever come to perfection. A hagiography that should have been a hanging.

What is the truth after all? It's what most people believe is the truth, whether it's a lie or not. When necessary, men can spin lies like spiders spin webs.

Men Usually Have a Plan

This is something you can count on. We never go into anything without a plan, at least some kind of plan. This is not to say it will be a good plan, or that it will work, or even make any sense, but you can believe at least we thought of *something*. Sometimes it's a scheme, or other times just a crazy idea. But the point is that at least we've got *something* in mind. There's a target of sorts, way off in the distance there. We're not just wandering around.

Every single "thing" was just an idea once. Chairs, pencils, glasses, electricity, light bulbs, trains, planes, cars, whatever you can think of really. Every "accomplishment" began as a possibility before it became a reality. And this is kind of an example of men at their best. Coming up with crazy plans and then acting on them. Turning whisps of ideas into actual things.

Bank robbers have plans. And most bank robbers are men by the way. You can look it up. Bonnie and Clyde were the exception, not the rule. But it proves my point. Even if it's a terrible idea, and one that will put the guy in prison should it fail, he didn't walk into that bank with no idea what he was doing there. He did come up with something. At least there's that. I think we can all agree that it's an incredibly stupid idea to rob a bank but at least if you're going to try it, have a plan to get in, get out and drive away.

How's about Christopher Columbus. I know that a lot of people now think he was some Italian kid who had an interesting idea, but damn. Talk about a plan. You can just imagine him with Queen Isabella… "So, your Highness. I have this idea. You give me some money. I will use it to buy three boats, hire 100 criminals, and we will travel three thousand miles and create a new trade route… to China! Yes, that's my plan." Well, whadayaknow, she bought it. Gave him the funds he required, bought him the boats, provided the salaries for all his pirates, and despite the fact that nothing he planned came to be, who cares now? The world is a different place as a result of His Plan.

No matter what else we do, men always try to have a plan. Not always a good one. Not always a smart one. Not always one that will work. But that's beside the point, isn't it? At least there was a plan.

Duct Tape

Duct Tape. One of the greatest of all inventions! Right up there with reading glasses, the chair, ESPN, and of course, a Dustbuster. Where would we be as a society without all these things, but especially without Duct Tape. It repairs what can't be repaired. It adds years of life to an otherwise piece of worthless nothing. It binds together anything that needs to be bound together to anything else. Rain, sleet or snow, doesn't matter. When it comes down to it, if one of us is looking for a solution to a problem, we often don't need to look much further than Duct Tape because there is not much else to see. In the wise words of Ken Shepard, a wise man from Louisiana and father of Kenny Wayne Shepard, "If something can't be fixed with Duct Tape then maybe it just can't be fixed."

Doesn't that perfectly describe men and how we approach a problem? And what we might sometimes call our reasoning? Isn't that exactly how a lot of us think? Aren't we just one shortcut from a perfect solution? And what better shortcut than duct tape? When in doubt, wrap a problem in something strong that can't be seen through and wait to see what happens. Who knows, maybe it'll fix itself. And if it doesn't, at least we can say we tried… Duct tape is the simplest and most likely solution to a lot of problems. And that's all we're really looking for. Solutions. And when in doubt, more duct tape.

Some Things Men Cannot Do

In addition to having no idea how to understand what women want, which we don't, and never have and likely never will, there are several other things men cannot figure out how to do. No matter how hard we try.

Generally speaking, without our navigation app, we cannot get from point a to point b. We will wander/drive/stumble around for several minutes or even hours before asking anyone where we are. If one of you asks one of us if we're lost, we will never admit it, as has been our custom and tradition for centuries.

We cannot listen. At least not yet. We have people in the research department trying to figure this out because we know it's very important. But until they tell us how to listen, we pretend that we are listening so that whoever is talking will think we are actually hearing the words coming out of their mouths. But really we have no idea how to master the art of listening, especially if there's a TV going. And I think we can all agree on that. Wait. What was I saying? The Dodger game is on...

We cannot remember important dates, like anniversaries of weddings and engagements and such. The more important they are, the more likely it is we will forget them. It's not personal, we just don't have a mechanism to keep good track. There's too many! Especially with wives and kids and such. Thankfully Mother's Day is such a big deal and there are so many reminders to get something special done for all the moms in our lives. Without all those commercials and banner ads we would get in big trouble every year.

We cannot dispose of old things. Clothing, such as underwear and socks and ties, we might keep around like they're antiques. And shoes too. We might have shoes that are older than our children. But we keep them, nonetheless. We also love to maintain ownership of unread books, old records and CD's, trophies, neon signs, tools, silverware and half-used candles. Not sure why but we hate to get rid of anything. I have no explanation why. It's an is.

We cannot shut up. We will say things that don't need to be said. We will offer suggestions that don't need to be suggested or ask not-pregnant women when their baby is due. We will whisper something under our breath that carries all the way across crowded rooms. I once heard a drunk guest at a wedding mention that a bride had too much make-up on at the exact moment the organist stopped playing

"The Wedding March." Whoops. But in truth, men get into more trouble because of their mouths than any other organ. Yes, even that one. From about age three on, the mouth is a source of nothing but trouble, and it never stops being a source of trouble. Grown ass men step blindly and confidently into huge piles of shizzle more often than not because they just thought of something hilarious and have to share it with the guy next to them. How can it be that we never learn? So prevalent is this crisis that every culture has some centuries old saying that underscores the point. Whether Italian, French, Spanish, Russian or Chinese, there is some proverb that boils down to, "Just shut the f*** up!!" Not that any of us ever listened to this sage advice, even if it was offered to us millions of times over thousands of years in hundreds of languages. Why shut up? What fourteen-year-old ever shuts up...?

So let's agree that the list of things men cannot do is probably endless and there are new entries all the time. But I have to get on with things.

A Man's Lifelong Mystery

How does a woman actually fall in love with one of us? How is it even possible that a woman could do this? Surely if they are as smart as they are beautiful, they can see that we are just 14 years old way down deep, and that we approach everything that matters in life and love as adolescents who are just guessing most of the time. Women have to know that we're just children, pretending. It's so obvious, right? We do nothing to hide it. We know in our heart of hearts that we are this way, pretending that we are all grown up but knowing that we are not. The idea that an adult woman, with knowledge and genius and an actual driver's license, could fall for one of us is so preposterous we can hardly believe it when it happens, no matter how many times it happens. These are women who have a view of the world that we will never have. They have careers, degrees, and reputations to uphold. They can actually create a life inside themselves. The idea that one of them would want to throw in with one of us is, frankly, ridiculous. How could she do it? Is she really not aware of what she's in for?

If one of us is filthy rich and promises a life of palaces and bodyguards and chinchilla throw rugs all over the place, okay that makes some sense. Or if we happen to be an heir without a care in the world, sure I get it. But what about the rest of us, the normal ones, the everyday guys, the scions of nobody special, the descendants of the everyday mom and dad types who have not changed the world at all. How do those kinds of guys not only have a girlfriend or two but then meet and marry an actual adult woman? It's crazy I know but there it is. *We don't know why women do this.* It makes no sense at all, at all. This is not to say we are not absolutely thrilled that they do, we just don't know how it happens and how it keeps happening.

Is it the way we dress? The new cologne? The shoes? Possibly the way we glide across a dance floor…? Is it the tooth whitening we finally decided to get done? The new suit? Do women feel that way about us because we're funny? Kind to strangers? Nice to waiters? Good providers, great storytellers, maybe because we speak a little French? What is it for God sakes? Is it that we have an old dog who still hangs around? Or a cat? Or an ex-wife possibly? Or what exactly? WE HAVE NO IDEA!! We just keep guessing and guessing until one of you falls for it.

Men Love to Punch Above Their Weight

One way men deal with the conundrum of women is very simple. As is practically everything we do, right? Basically, it comes down to this: If you, the woman, are attractive enough to be completely out of our league, yet you seem to like us, even just a little, then game on. Let's GOOOO! We're yours – like a lost puppy finding a new home. Come claim your prize. You want some of this? You got it. You want one of us? You got us. If you're really interested, and you're even slightly better looking than we could have ever imagined, then we're really interested too. It's that easy. If you're gorgeous in any way, and you're into one of us, then we're in. Body and soul. In most wedding pictures have you noticed that the guy looks completely surprised? He's likely asking himself, "What the hell am I doing here? I ran into this super cute girl at an Erewhon, made her laugh a couple of times, and next thing I know I'm standing here in a tuxedo in front of all my friends making a bunch of promises I never thought I'd ever make!" And that's that.

Men don't have the time, energy or maturity to challenge what's there right under our noses. A woman beyond our dreams who finds us interesting is all we need to hit the Let's Do This! button. We will never understand how this all works anyway, nor know just why it keeps happening, but we don't have to, do we? We will love the girl who loves us, especially if she is cuter than we are handsome. Which is easy enough since most of us know we basically look like hell most of the time anyway.

Is this shallow? Yes of course it's shallow! Is this immature? Yes of course it's immature. But remember what you're dealing with here. An adolescent boy.

A fourteen-year-old. Who, for whatever reason, is ready, willing and dying to be and become your complete soul mate. Just be cute, choose him, let him know in some unforgettable way that you're available, and he's all in.

The rest of his life he will be swinging for the fences and living the dream. Thanks in large part to you letting him pretend to be a player in a game of love that he has no business being in. He's punching above his weight and doesn't even know it.

What You See Is What You Get

It would be a much simpler and gentler world for men if the rest of the world would simply recognize the cold, hard and often disappointing fact that we are lousy at changing. Okay, let me say it another way: We do not change. It's a bad word for us. Unless we're talking about a golf swing. That could always be a little better. But other things, especially important things, nope. Not gonna do it, not gonna happen. I could say "we will never ever change at all" but that would make us sound like we are stuck in the mud. Which we are for the most part, but I don't want any readers (like my friend Kate) to toss this book out the window just because I'm being truthful.

Change is not good for us. Change is difficult and frightening. Change is pretty much impossible. When we look at ourselves, we see a relatively finished portrait. Repeat, relatively finished. Okay, maybe we need to lose a little weight, or trim our nose hairs, or get a new suit, or quit chewing with our mouths open, but other than these sorts of minor imperfections, we honestly believe we're done. If someone wants to change us, that means they don't think we're as done as we would like to believe. We cannot survive in a world that wants to change the who we have struggled so mightily to become.

Every Man's Three Basic Requirements

I know what you're thinking… Food, Sex and Beer. Or Cigars, Sex and Food. Or Sex, Sex and Sex. Whatever you're thinking, it's not what you're thinking.

Now, I don't know how many basic requirements women must have to be happy. It's probably a lot. But being a dude, I really have no idea what those might be or how long the list is. On the other hand, I know that most men have just three basic requirements in order to participate in something, at least willingly. And if these can be met, most men would be agreeable to whatever the plan happens to be from that point on.

First and foremost, there has to be some **FUN** in whatever it is we're supposed to be doing. At some point in the task, we have to be able to have a good time doing whatever it is. Whether working, doing the taxes, playing, relaxing, driving, cooking, traveling, whatever. There has to be some happiness there somewhere. So if you can make it fun on some level, we will be there, sitting up straight, ready to go!

Secondly, there has to be some **APPRECIATION**. Without proper recognition of our efforts at whatever it is we are undertaking our hearts are empty. The results are then meaningless. This is particularly true when it comes to the people who are on the trip with us. We need to hear it from our partners. They (ie you the reader) have to tell us when you notice the good things we're doing. That you recognize how much work we are doing to keep the family happy or the bank account full. Just notice us!! We will bloom like new roses. This will work over and over too.

Lastly, there has to be some **REWARD** for our efforts. This is not to say we need a medal every time we take out the trash or run a good meeting, but you might try to think of something…? A couple of Reese's Peanut Butter cups next to a hot coffee go a long way. Or a cold beer sweating as it waits for us to finish some awful task works well. Or some form of payment. Money is always a good way to show appreciation to the young man in your life. Cash is better but checks and Venmo work too.

Just being aware of these three basic requirements puts you way ahead of the crowd on this critical point.

Our Gift to Humanity

Of all the contributions made by all the men to the world, and there are many, there is one that really stands out. Without this particular gift we, and I mean all of humanity here, we all would be less human. Without it we would be less alive. Without it we would be less ourselves, less civilized, and would probably have become something far more barbaric. Not talking about boats or gunpowder or cellphones or satellites, or any of those sorts of things. Those are all great, but… Man's great gift to humanity is Pets. That's right. Pets. Those precious furry things that like to tear apart your best loafers and then sit in the middle of the living room licking their butts. They are completely innocent until proven guilty, which they never are, because they have no sense of guilt.

It was a man who discovered the concept of "pet" when one of us first encouraged a curious beast to cross the line of danger and join him at the fire. It was some hairy and smelly fellow who somehow had the foresight to see that a friendly wild animal was far better for the tribe than an attacking and angry wild animal. According to NationalGeo.Com (and those two mouse clicks represent some voracious research on my part), man's first pets were wolves. Vicious, teeth-baring, annoyed and growling wolves. They introduced themselves by feeding on the garbage left behind by our forebears that were crisscrossing Europe and Asia 30,000 years ago or so.

As time went on, they became part of the tribes. The wolves grew less and less aggressive, and some outliers eventually evolved into dogs. Soon the wolves/dogs were being bred to help with hunting and herding and guarding the tribe. Many, many years later (like now actually), they are being bred to be cute and cuddly enough to win first prize at the New York Kennel Club Dog Show. That's quite a journey isn't it?

For you cat lovers, alongside the dog-as-pet development, the first successful hunter-gatherers created grain storage units for all the nuts and berries they found. But the granaries attracted rats and other pests. So these prescient geniuses discovered that the best way to get rid of them was to invite a host of carnivorous felines who lived nearby to move in and feast on all the rodents. So these wise boys did the same thing with cats that those wandering tribes did with dogs.

So just think. Men did this. They pulled it off. They imagined the impossible and then put it into action. They had a plan. They turned wild animals into harmless pals! And where would humanity be without its pets? No dogs barking and yipping and jumping all over the place when you get home. No cats stretched across your best clothes? No birds chirping all day. No hamsters, no rabbits, no guinea pigs, no snakes! No. None of them would be part of our daily lives if not for a gentle-hearted (and probably very smelly) dude, thousands of years ago, who invited a wolf to join him and his family for dinner at the campfire.

I bring up this point as an insight into what men are really all about. As an illustration of what man, or men, are like when left to their own devices and instincts. We are basically just nice guys, looking for accomplices, anywhere we can find them. We are welcoming of strangers, deserving or otherwise, and like to try turning them into friends. We are especially kindhearted and nice to animals, especially if they are not trying to eat us. So, if you're running out of reasons to like or love one of us, remember that we are the descendants of great men, fearless men, extraordinary men. And we have taken that noble birthright and evolved it into what you see today: a big fraternity of mostly overgrown teenagers, running around, running wild, sometimes running companies and running countries. But thanks to a few of our kind, there is a lot more happiness in the world, a lot more contentment in billions of lives, and a lot less space in millions of apartments. You're welcome, planet.

PART 2

Men Compared to Women

Much has been published about the similarities and differences between men and women. Men Are From Mars, Women Are From Venus comes to mind. Everything You Wanted to Know About Sex covers the subject too.

So, we can all agree that everybody loves and dreams and eats and drinks, but right after that, all bets are off. This because almost everything men do their way, women do another way. Practically everything. Men think about things one way, and women might not even think about those things at all. And vice versa of course. Men can sometimes see the value of women's different habits and practices, but it's rare.

Women often care little about men's unique way of looking at things because they're too busy and know by now that most men are just immature children anyway.

Here are some of the many differences between men and women.

If Men and Women Were Airplanes

If women and men were airplanes instead of human beings, women would be fully loaded F-14 fighter jets. Men would be a piece of paper folded over a couple of times held together with a piece of scotch tape.

That to say that yes, men are that simple, and yes, women are that complicated, at least according to me and the fourteen-year-old boy who's helping me write this. Just ask any man what women really want and a stupid look will come across his face. "I have no idea," will be his likely answer. That's how complicated women appear to be to men. It's like the directions are written in another language. And just when we think we are starting to figure it out, a new update arrives and we are back to the starting point again. Even if this is a relationship that is not brand new, we still are clueless. Ask a woman what men want and there's a good chance she will nod knowingly and say, "Sex and beer." And she might not be that far off.

As I've mentioned and repeated a few times now, men are simple beings, easy to understand and very predictable. Sure we want families and career success and approbation and club memberships but what we really want is an uncomplicated life, where we please our partners and ourselves, and get to the end of it without ever having to give up our fourteen-year-old boy dreams. Okay, some sex and some beer too, or their basic equivalents, depending on the individual, but that's just an exemplar of the life we're trying to figure out.

I cannot begin to say what women want because first and foremost I wouldn't begin to presume, and secondly, I'm a dude so honestly I know nothing about it anyway. Like most if not all of us men, I stumble forward on the path of life and hope I get more things right than I get wrong.

Women Have Emotions,
Men Have Reactions

Women, at least as far as I can tell, have a range of nuanced responses and complex emotional replies to most everything that happens. Women's lives are substantive, and rich with detail, and most things they experience inspire a different *feeling*. Almost everything in a woman's life seems to have an emotion attached to it. Furnishings and fabrics elicit feelings, as do movies and books and tv shows. The right clothes can earn a bit of a shiver too, and even food makes some women emote. Have you ever heard a guy say, "Fellas… Charlie's Broccoli Surprise is UNREAL!!" No. And you won't either.

Men would give more in this area but our emotional equipment hasn't been fully installed yet. We're still waiting for the technician to show up and do some more tests, check the wiring and solder a few more connections. So, as a result, men have just a few options when it comes to their reactions. When you get down to it, we only have three ways to feel about anything. Happy. Sad. Angry. That's right, and that's all we got. Which is why men are much more simplistic about what they feel things about. Where women have a rainbow of emotional choices, men basically have a black and white television from the early fifties, with a red stripe in the middle of the screen.

Women have emotions like Crayola has crayons. Men have a stubby pencil. When it comes to their emotions, women get to see the Mona Lisa every day and we get to see Snoopy.

If our favorite team wins the Super Bowl or the World Cup, then we're out dancing in the streets and hugging complete strangers, maybe for an hour or two, a day at most. But right after that storm calms down, we're back to basics. If a stock blows up and brings in some real dosh, we might react with a fist bump and a chortle. No mas. It's not that big a deal. Nothing is really that big a deal. Unless we get angry and then everything's a big deal. If by chance some ass-hole should scratch the paint or door dent our new car, we might hunt them down like prey and come close to murder. If we have been wronged, or have been the victim of a theft, that grudge might last a lifetime or beyond. We actually might send our kids to make amends if we're no longer around. We're that primordial. Other than the occasional celebration, or the tears shed if we lost a good dog or a best friend, we are just who we are: dudes. Emotionally speaking, there's up, down and a little sideways. And that's pretty much it in terms of directions. We're like a three-piece jigsaw puzzle. Easy to put together and just as easy to take apart. We do not need a lot of emotions to get through our lives. And we don't worry about all that's missing emotionally speaking because we don't need to feel that many feelings just to get through a day. Black, white, red...

Men feel strongly about a few things, of course, but not *everything*. We care deeply about our families, our money, our sports, maybe a hobby or two, but that's where the road ends. That's pretty much the whole entire list. All that we have to offer, emotionally speaking, is on display all the time. It's right then and right there, right in front of us for the whole world to see. We wear our hearts on our sleeves because we don't know where else to put them. We're not shallow by choice, that's just how deep the water is.

It happens this way because we have a very basic way of looking at most things. Simpler than most of the women in our lives anyway. Something is right or wrong. Good or bad. A woman loves us or she doesn't. The shoes fit or they don't. It's daytime or nighttime. These kinds of determinations are easy to make. Not a lot of thinking, not a lot of intrigue. Just the recognition of the most obvious facts. And this extends into all aspects of our existence. To us, the color of the wall is not beige or russet or raw umber or chocolate. It's *brown*, okay? The food tastes good, or it sucks. The comedian made us laugh or she didn't. A simpler existence unfolds before us because we don't force what few emotions we have available into all aspects of our lives. Who needs all those extra things to consider just to decide if there's enough time to take a nap before poker?

A songwriter I worked with for many years finally had a big hit song. It turned out to be a worldwide #1 that would ensure his place in history and his fortunes along with it. When he realized the full scope of his remarkable accomplishment, he turned to me and said, "Well, it's about time…" Not bouncing off the walls or bounding down to his local bar, not filling his tiny closet with new clothes, not really all that emotional at all. Like I mentioned, all he felt was right there for all to see.

Emotionally speaking, women paint master-pieces that might hang in museums someday; their feelings are that rich. Men draw in the dirt with a blunt stick. The most simplistic and basic approach to things is fine for most of us. Who needs all that minutia? What good are a slew of emotions when it comes to living a perfect life? We don't need all the nonsense. We have an experience, make a decision about what it is or is not, and then try to find a cold beer and figure out what we're going to do next.

Men Count Each Other's Money, Women Count Each Other's Wrinkles

Being competitive is part of the foundation of human nature, going back to our days running from hungry predators and getting into the cave ahead of all the others. The hairy Neanderthals who survived were able to pass along their gifts for speed and agility and all the other traits that gave them that winning competitive edge. Which allows those of us, their lucky descendants, to sit here complacently at the top of the food chain and live these beautiful lives.

The competition is no less fierce today than it was back then. But we compete for different versions of survival now. For men today, the competition begins and ends with things. The houses, the cars, the watches and the joys of having more toys than the next guy. What fuels that drive are the careers we get to have, the size of the companies we get to work for, the clubs we get to be members of and if we're lucky, the bonuses we get at the end of the year. As Tom Cruise likes to say over and over in Jerry McGuire, "Show me the money!" Ultimately it is all about the money when it comes to how men keep score. Money funds a man's sense of self-worth and as well his sense of self. And this is how a man measures himself against the other men. (Wow. That got kinda serious all of a sudden...)

Women play the same game. Just as competitive, just as much keeping score, just as much "Me vs. Them." But for women it's not about the money. It's all about the beauty. Who looks better than whom? Who looks younger than whom? Who catches more vibe than whom? And on and on it goes, day and night. How a woman looks compared to the other women is the daily battle. Best Dressed. Best Hair. Best Shoes. Fewest Wrinkles. Least amount of "Work." And so on. You want evidence? Recall Megan Kelly accosting Jane Fonda about a possible facelift, live on national TV? It was a wow moment. Jane Fonda looked great, and not just for her age, she just looked great. And Megan Kelly tried to take her down because of it, plain and simple. That moment displayed the true underbelly of the competition that exists between women for all to see.

You want more evidence? How's this. According to Statista.com, the worldwide fashion and apparel business for women was worth $927B in 2024. The worldwide cosmetic business was worth $765B in 2024, with 96% of that purchased by women. The worldwide women's haircare business was valued at $80B in 2024. Add those three numbers together, it's $1.772 Trillion. Divide that number by 2.25B (the number of women who will be on the planet between the ages of 15 and 70 in 2025 according to the U.N.), and the total amount of money that will be spent worldwide is about $1250 per adult woman per year. That's the whole world. The same statistics for just America alone equal almost $2500 per adult woman per year. No matter how you smear it that's a lot of mascara!

And why is all this cash going out? For the men? To impress all the dudes a woman might see during her day? Awww hell no. We're not even allowed to notice women anymore, much less watch them as they walk by. A compliment misconstrued could easily cost one of us our jobs and erase our present and deny our future. So what that means is that basically women are getting dolled up each and every day for two simple reasons. First, to impress all the other women they might see, plain and simple. Second, to look a helluva lot better than all the other women they might see will look.

What I'm saying here is that we all count something. Men count the moola, women count the grooves...

Man Law Is Nothing Compared to Girl Code

I've always known about Man Law, a staple of every boy's existence and survival. But I had never even heard of Girl Code until recently. Who knew women had a code all worked out? And don't even ask how I got this information. It was difficult to unearth and involved a lot of begging and over-tipping my son's babysitter. I even pretended not to write down what I was writing down when she started talking about it. I expect that there will be calls for an investigation into the leak that allowed this data to go public, and I will probably get hauled in front of some congressional committees but I'm okay with that. It was worth it and shows my commitment to the truth!!

As with all the differences between us fourteen-year-olds and the women in our lives, the man's side is uncomplicated and the women's side is not at all. I'm not going to compare point by point, because there are not enough points to make on the man's side and way too many on the woman's side. And the babysitter might have been lying anyway. But here's what I learned.

Man Law is as simple as simple can be, just like us. Under its basic terms, a man must never do anything that will make another man look bad in front of the woman he is currently associated with, living with, sexing with or even sexting with. That's it. That's Man Law. Don't ever mess with another dude's personal situation. Expanded Man Law, I.e. the broader application of the basic law is: Never make a man look bad in front of any woman, period. The exception is if two men are competing for the same woman, then all bets are off and it's like a jousting tournament in Elizabethan England. Grab your lance and let the games begin!

Girl Code apparently has several key features, but there are also many facets and nuances mixed in, as needed for any particular scenario. There are standards, and then there are details and departures from the standards. By far the most revealing thing is that Girl Code can change from group to group. What's acceptable in one pod of women might be completely unacceptable in the one just down the street. Each group of girls loosely establishes the rules they vow to follow to keep their coterie of friendships alive. So here are some of the key elements of Girl Code, at least as I have been able to ascertain.

1. Lying is okay, because girls lie all the time. (This is *not* my opinion but is based on a discussion I had with the babysitter's sister in a follow up interview at a nearby Bagel Nosh.)

2. No sleeping with another girl's ex, *unless* she set you up or she introduced you to him. (But there is a flexible one-year window on this rule.)

3. Indiscriminate behavior (ie, slutty) is okay! It makes the bad girls look worse, but makes the good girls look better.

4. No hiding pertinent information about a man, his habits or his peculiarities, especially if a friend in the pod is about to go out with or sleep with him.

5. If two girls are in love with the same man, *neither of them* can get with him without the other girl's blessing. If neither concedes, he's off limits.

6. Never ever leave another girl behind, whether at a bar or a party or most decidedly at some dude's house, especially if she's been drinking.

7. Share incriminating details about a man's "private" behavior so that everyone in the pod can learn and benefit from that knowledge.

8. Be completely honest with the other girls about how they look.

9. Treat all the other girls like you would want them to treat you, unless you don't feel like it or they were rude to you in the bathroom.

10. When dealing with men, refer to Rule #1 and don't hesitate to tell however many lies are necessary.

Let me just say, on behalf of all the boys, that I was pretty much shell-shocked when I realized that women had all these intense guidelines and men had drawn a couple of lines in the sand. My reaction then and now is a combination of "Really?!?" and "Are you kidding me!" Women talk about us, and what we do and how we do it, and share all those details with each other…? *Sacre Bleu!!* (I just realized I know so much French I should have my own cooking show…) Finding out that women actually have a code, albeit an incredibly flexible and fungible one, was like finding out the other team had actually been practicing for the big game while us boys were just hanging out at the park.

Men don't have a plan when it comes to women. Every day is new and every relationship is newer, even if it's very much the same as all that came before. We don't share information about girls we've known unless we are absolutely forced to do so. This is because we might be getting back together with her someday, if she ever calls back. Yes, we try to always back each other up and never make another guy look bad, if it can be avoided, but other than that, it's a competition to the death. It's just the way we roll. That's what *mano a mano* means. (I think so anyway, I don't have time to look all this stuff up!)

Man Law vs. Girl Code. Further incontrovertible evidence of the fundamental, impossible, unchangeable, and remarkable differences between us fourteen-year-old boys and the women we're trying to pretend we're grownups around.

Women Want Compliments, Men Need Praise

All of us like to be acknowledged. Whether we made our stockholders a few billion dollars or kept the house as clean as a museum. Whether we made a great putt to win a golf tournament or got the family together for holiday dinner without a fight breaking out over politics. Whatever it was, whoever we are, we all want to know that we were noticed. Toiling away without the right kind of recognition is no fun at all.

But as with most things, the type of acknowledgement that satisfies is a very different thing for men and for women.

Women, at least in the limited way I understand things about women, really love to be complimented. They like their compliments on a constant and regular basis. Whether for how brilliant an idea is or how smart a decision was, how well they met the challenges of the stockholder meeting or how they met the expectations of the boss or

93

whatever miracle they just pulled off. Whether for how nice they look, how their hair falls or how good they smell, or whatever it is. Women seem to enjoy a stream of compliments to wash over them with steady regularity, like a warm shower. As long as they are truthful and honest compliments that is. BS is BS and nobody wants that.

Men are not interested in a stream of little compliments. We interrupt these kinds of exercises with a wince and a hand wave. We expect ourselves to be good at everything anyway, so someone's acknowledgement that we did what is expected of us is not interesting. And besides, what good are some little compliments gonna do for us and our voracious egos? Really, very little. What we need is something much bigger and stronger. We want to be *Praised* for our efforts, and that's praised with a capitol *P*.

The need for praise is why so many guys do the things they do but especially why men golf. Getting praised by the others in your foursome is a big part of the camaraderie of the game. "GREAT *PUTT* ROGER!!" "Fantastic SHOT Ricky!!" "I want to drive like you when I grow up Richard!!" These are the kinds of things that golfers shout at each other throughout the round. It's Big Praise for Big Boys!! Talk about getting recognized. Just see what happens when one of us gets a Hole-in-One. Whoa boy, easy now. You get a plaque to take home and your picture in the club's newsletter! What I'm trying to say is that golf gets a man the praise he craves!

So now that you have a better understanding of what you're dealing with, how does this inside knowledge apply to a normal everyday situation with a man in your life? It's easy. If we clean up the yard, we need to know it is the greatest yard clean up in the history of yards and the history of cleaning them. If we ever get around to painting the guest room, we would appreciate you comparing our work to Michelangelo and the ceiling of the Sistine Chapel. If we go to a boring but necessary party, like your High School Reunion for instance, and we happen to stay sober and act charming the whole night, and do not punch your drunk ex-boyfriend in the face, we need to hear it from you loud and clear that it was the greatest acting performance since Joaquin Phoenix won his Oscar for The Joker.

Suppose one of us does something that really is deserving of unending praise, like firemen do every day, or rescue-dog shelter owners do every minute, or like thoughtful strangers do helping stranded motorists. Or just suppose we do something unbelievably heroic or extremely thoughtful, like all the first responders do whenever they do anything. Well alrighty then, let the praise begin and never end!

Men Are Not Complicated,
Women Not So Much

Men are not complicated. At all. We are simple creatures, equipped with just a few natural defense mechanisms. We look at the world in the same way any fourteen-year-old boy would, which is to say we know who and what we are most of the time, and we know who and what we are absolutely not, again, most of the time. We know what is ours and we know when we need to steal something. We know what a lie feels like and we don't like ourselves so much after we tell one, but we know that to keep up the myth we will have to slip a few in. We know love because it is the only thing that feels better than anything else we know. We are not necessarily whiners, as a rule, but it is a readily available tool in the toolbox. Sometimes we are selfish, yes, and sometimes prideful too. But we can be talked out of that kind of behavior easily enough. Usually a quick punch with a closed fist will do it.

We are sometimes jealous, and usually much more than we need to be. We are also revengeful on occasion, and also way more than we need to be. But we try to be honest and hardworking, diligent and truthful. We do not mind long hours, or difficult work, or coaching sports teams, or helping raise the children, or unplugging smelly clogged drains. We lift heavy things and walk dogs. Oftentimes, we can be charming with our least appreciative in-laws, as long as there is limited exposure and plenty of warning in advance. Yes, we have basic physical requirements, but they are, for the most part, pretty easy to understand and satisfy. In other words, again, not complicated.

Women get fed up with men being so uncomplicated because women are so much more complicated than men are. I think women get bored with their men sometimes because it's the same thing over and over, day after day, stretching into year after year.

Women operate on several levels, often at the same time. They are quick to extract nuance from every detail. They are ready to question and discuss practically anything at length. They are willing to talk, and work things out. And not only do they want to understand the problem, whatever it is, they want to be understood when they're discussing its solution. They really want to be listened to. And because they are more emotionally grounded

than men, women can feel deeply about almost anything, whether pets or movies or friends with broken hearts, like they're flicking a switch. Oh yeah,
and women actually read the directions when they
buy things!

Men don't read the directions. And men don't
really want to spend a lot of time talking about
things when they can just rush in blindly and try a
quick fix. Men just want to make problems go away.

Men can care deeply about a few things, like
family, friends, money, a favorite team and of course
whatever is supposed to be happening tomorrow. But
after those points are covered, that's it. Everything
else is in the weeds and we don't like to get lost in
the weeds. (This all sounds really naïve, doesn't it?
Who's writing this book anyway, a child? Oh, wait,
I forgot. A child *is* writing this book.)

Men Rule the World and They Are Destroying It. How Might Women Rule the World?

Ever heard of Ellen Johnson Sirleaf? Want to talk about an extraordinary person who has made a real and positive difference in the lives of millions and millions of people? She has to be part of the discussion. She was the first woman democratically elected as a head of state in Africa, when she became President of Liberia in 2006. Previous to her election, that country had witnessed not one but two civil wars which killed over 250,000 of her countrymen. During her first term Liberia was ground zero in the Ebola epidemic, when another 13,000 souls were lost. She handled that with relative smoothness somehow and then managed to erase $5 billion in national debt, attract $18b in international investment, and win the Nobel Peace Prize. She then won the Ibrahim Prize, recognizing the fact that she had organized the first peaceful transition of power in Liberia in 75 years. And perhaps most importantly, she kept her country out of war for one of the longest stretches in its history. Liberia was founded by freed slaves in 1847 and had been in one fight or another almost every year since. Ellen Sirleaf is the living embodiment of the Tupac Shakur poem, "The Rose That Grew from the Concrete." Out of the broken society she inherited, she created peace and wealth and prosperity, bringing a breath of hope to her country and its populace.

There are not many examples of people like her. And who knows when the next gracious, generous and thoughtful peace-loving leader will make it to the top position of his or her country and lead it with the same genius and kindness as she did.

As it stands presently, men have been ruling the world for five millenniums, give or take a couple of centuries here and there. Very few women have gotten a chance to show what they can do with such a grand opportunity, other than the outliers. Ellen Johnson Sirleaf, Angela Merkel, Indira Ghandi, Golda Meir, Cleopatra, Helen of Troy, and very few others. Maybe Joan of Arc had an angle but she scared the hell out of all the men and got burned at the stake at 19 before she could make her full impact.

During the years men have been in charge, our history as a people has been marked by nothing if not conflict, territoriality, despots and dictators, and disputes that last for hundreds of years. We have endless wars, while hurling futile accusations, and bring unending suffering to all involved. Men make both a habit and practice of allowing themselves to be engaged and enraged over the antagonistic actions and impossible demands of the other men and then refuse to budge an inch in order to let things just settle down.

Men apparently like war and start new ones all the time. What is amazing is that none of the previous wars ever made the world any more peaceful, yet that is always the stated intent. Over and over again men lead other men and boys into carnage after carnage, always promising peace. But at the end of the day what do they have to show for all the smoke and blood and armor and explosions? Surprisingly little. When it's all said and done, other than another medal on another chest, and more human treasure lost in cold graveyards, there is not much to show at all. The longest war in our country's history was the one in Afghanistan. It was sold to an unsuspecting American public based on the vital importance of ridding the world of warlords who were using their dirt as a platform to wreak havoc. So intent were our leaders on starting this war that none of them actually went to the trouble of verifying if there were any real threats that they had claimed were so dangerous to the world. And when it turned out, inevitably, that there were not, all the generals said was "Whoops!" and shouldered on ahead anyway.

So let's ask ourselves, who would do something so stupid as to start a war? Who could be that oblivious of the consequences? Who would completely overlook the sacrifice and effort required to invade, destroy and re-build a nation? Who would think a task of such enormity could work? Who would rush to battle, foolishly declaring victory no matter what is really going on? Ummm, let's see. Would the answer happen to be a bunch of boys pretending to be men while unashamedly exercising their fourteen-year old instincts? Would *they* be the type of people who would rely on snippets of truth and tons of military bluster to make world changing decisions? Yes! They would and they did. That's what would happen and that's what did happen.

But is the world any safer for these childish actions? These sacrifices? The loss of all those men and women and civilians and everything else? Is the world really a better place to be? And what do we have to show for all our trouble? The Afghanistan War effort cost the U.S. $2.3 TRILLION and ended the lives of 176,000 people. It was a terrible waste that serves to illustrate perfectly the vast differences

in men and women's approaches to issues and problems. It reveals why women are actually much better
equipped to run the world. Although men hate it
when women do it, women have the ability to step
back and say, BEFORE they jump, Hey there...
Wait a minute. Maybe we should look at this situation again just one more time, before we do something really stupid, like start a war...

Call me crazy but, if the world was ruled by
women, I cannot imagine them all getting together
and saying that the only solution to all the intracta-
ble problems we face today (and have always faced
by the way) is to send our children into battle to kill
someone else's children. And every few years to try it
again, and again, and again. And even though it has
ABSOLUTELY NEVER worked before, just keep
trying, just in case it might work this time. Isn't the
definition of insanity to do the same thing over and
over and hope that there will be a different result?
Maybe I'm naïve but I just don't see all the women
in the world getting together and handling it in that
insane a way....

One of the biggest problem men have (and usually do not realize they have it) is that they rush in
blindly to almost everything. They show up with a
handful of band-aids or hand grenades, whichever
is closer, and try to fix a problem before they even
know what it really is. They rely on the same four-

teen-year year old pimply-faced boy logic they have always relied on when making big decisions. And this usually makes things much worse. Men crave the sweat of conflict while women shy from it. Men are the generals who send their troops into battle knowing many will die, while women are often the nurses who wait behind the battle lines to care for the injured and bury the dead. Neither men nor women are that much better for the experience, but who learns more?

If we started over today, and let women run the world, I imagine it would probably be a remarkably peaceful place to live. There would be far less conflict and much less stupidity. Fewer wars. Less hubris. No reason to rely on pure force to make a point or win an argument. The air would not stink of testosterone, crumbled buildings and jet fighter fuel. There would be a greater degree of attention given to the importance of life and not the importance of death. Use of anger as a tool in every discussion would be way down, and use of logic in every decision would be way up.

But if we started over today and let men run the world, in no time at all it would be in exactly the same mess it's in right now. Ruling the world is not a representation of men at their finest, clearly. All that happens is war, and then another and another. And all that war leads to mayhem, chaos, loss of life and loss of innocence. And there's the aftermath to deal with before the next war begins. Rinse and repeat. And repeat. And repeat.

This is not to say that men can't rule other things, like businesses or sports teams, or fashion houses, or banks. But as far as running the whole goddamn world is concerned, I think that's women's work.

Men and Women Should Probably Not Shop Together

When shopping, men attack. Women browse. Men go into stores like hired assassins. They know exactly and precisely what they are going to buy. There is no wasted time. There are no other options but to buy just the thing they are there to buy. Find the item, get in line, pay, get back in the car, go home. They know what it is and where it is. They know the aisle the item is on and how far away from the cash register it is. They know down to the last minute how long it should take to find it, grab it, pay for it, and get the hell out of there and back to the important stuff (like the NBA rookie combine or a darts championship on ESPN 8 – The Ocho). Men have a period of time blocked out in their mind to finish the whole shopping operation. If they have to wait even a minute longer it starts to feel like hours, like standing on a tack barefoot. Watch a man in the checkout line. He'll have his item ready to be purchased and a few last minute indulgences, but not much more. He fidgets, checks his phone, taps his foot, and looks with evil intent at the sales associate manning the register. Until it's his turn. He's got the credit card ready and practically in his hand, he knows where to sign, and everything is go go go. Until he is back in the car and on the way home or on to the next assignation. Only then will he take a deep breath and relax. It's literally like a professional killer. In. Out. Gone. Next. No prisoners. No witnesses.

Women, on the other hand, approach shopping in a completely different way. And as different as men and women are in most categories, it is true in the way they shop as well. First thing women do in stores is take a deep breath, look around, and survey the task at hand. They aren't there to buy one thing, they are there to buy *anything*. Potentially anyway. They will lay down that credit card for whatever strikes their fancy or suits their eye, that moment and that day. If it's right, it's sold. If it tickles their intellect, it's practically on the wall or in the closet already. They might even forget why they went to that store in the first place. This is not criticism. It's fact.

Women don't shop for individual things so much as they shop for categories of things. Clothes, cleaning supplies, make-up, shoes... You rarely, if ever, see a woman walk out of a store with just one thing. It's not the way they like to acquire new stuff.

As long as they are in the store, just about every item in that store is a possible purchase. Women stroll in stores. They are like what the French call "flaneurs" which roughly translates to 'One who is not in a big hurry…" (Again with the French. Why, I'm almost fluent!) Women linger. Women think about things. Every aisle holds any number of mysteries waiting to unfold before them. They're like kids at Legoland. And here's why. (By the way it took me an entire lifetime to figure this out. You just get to sit back and read about it.) When women shop, it's not just an experience. It's a *creative* experience. Their imaginations are on high as they promenade through a store or mall or duty-free shop. A walk through the shoe aisle at Macy's is like Claude Monet taking a walk down by the River Seine. Women move through the aisles and let their thoughts fly. They might be asking themselves… What could I do with that? How would this look in the den? Where could I hang these? What kind of party could I wear these shoes to? How would I look in that dress? They try to imagine how any of the thousands of items in their purview would fit into their lives. They visualize themselves in or on, at or with, running or jumping, dancing or biking, or whatever else. This is true with anything they see. And it goes on and on like this in every store. Shopping for women is an act of intellectual stimulation. Men prefer their intellectual stimulation over a cold beer perusing the internet. Stores are for buying the one thing they need at that moment and then racing back home to see if it works. The only things men and women should shop for together are cars, beds, sofas and tv's.

29 Things Ordinary Men and Women Said About Men and Women

As a way of trying to completely understand the many differences between men and women, I conducted interviews with about 100 people. "Conducted" is probably too strong a word. How about "Chatted with." Yeah, better. Some were married, some were single, some were looking for Mr. Right or Mrs. Wrong. Some were tired of looking. Many were a little inebriated, since I was killing two birds with one stone and did a lot of my research in bars. Most everyone seemed to be extraordinarily willing to share their honest thoughts. All of them took it seriously and tried to answer the one question that I was looking for an answer to, and that was, "What is the *biggest* difference between men and women?"

Everyone I spoke with was promised complete anonymity, even if their spouse/girlfriend/boyfriend/

other was standing just ten feet away, so presumably all spoke freely. This promise also allowed most participants to be completely truthful, or at least somewhat truthful, or at least appear to be somewhat truthful. Like a small candle in a huge, dark cave, these answers shine a dim and tiny light into the chasm that exists between us. These are all direct quotes, by the way, though many were scrawled on cocktail napkins and might have gotten changed a little in translation, or got beer spilled on them and were then reconstructed by yours truly. But they are generally what you might expect. Men's answers are often indelicate and too straightforward, while women's answers are thoughtful insights you can actually learn something from. These are all direct quotes, though many were scrawled on cocktail napkins and might have changed a little in translation, or got beer spilled on them and were partially reconstructed by yours truly.

According to Men, the biggest difference between men and women is...

1. "Men are simple, blunt, direct and to the point. Women dance around the truth like Girl Scouts at a campfire."
2. "Men usually say what they are supposed to say, whether they believe it or not. Women

are usually not listening, so it doesn't matter anyway."

3. "Women have to discuss *everything*. Men don't want to discuss it, they just want to fix it. Or ignore it completely. In case it fixes itself."

4. "For women, perfect sex is something that happens at the right place at the right time, with the right person. Men can have perfect sex almost anytime. With just about anybody."

5. "What women gain in wisdom the skin of their neck loses in elasticity."

6. "Women compare men to their fantasies, imagining what a perfect man would be like, how thoughtful he would be and all that bs. Then they measure their own man against that image. It's a waste of time, lady!" The vastly overweight guy paused here and took a slosh of whatever he was drinking too much of, belched and continued, "Umm… What was I saying?"

7. "To a woman, romance is a short-term marketing campaign. For men, romance is what happens right up until the moment she starts to remind you of your mother."

8. "A woman always looks more beautiful right after she's come to her senses and broken off the relationship. Then, she's gorgeous."

9. "I don't know why, but women over-complicate everything. To balance things out, men over-simplify everything. Because of this, men sound like idiots and women look like geniuses."

10. "If a man swallowed a marble it would go right through him. If a woman swallowed a marble, you might never see it again."

11. "Relationships are like boxing. Men want to land the knockout; women like to counter punch. The man gives an idea its initial spark and leaves the woman to work out the details. Perfect example? Pregnancy."

12. "Men are intrigued by women who feel deeply about things like big causes and such, but only if she's kinda hot."

13. "The biggest difference between men and women is Viagra. It's the greatest recreational drug ever created."

14. "Face it, men are attracted to women who are attracted to them. It makes things a lot easier. But men are also very attracted to any woman who is dating their best friend. Like 'Jessie's Girl.'"

According to Women, the biggest difference is...

1. "Women can figure out any situation faster and more completely than men because men are basically clueless."

2. "Biggest difference? Men don't bathe enough. And they're stupid." Admittedly, the woman who offered this up was a little drunk and very upset with her "date" who was asleep and drooling on his Chicago Bears jersey.

3. "Men pretend to love us so they can have sex with us. So, in response, we pretend to have sex with them."

4. "Men are awful, just awful." I immediately regretted asking her to participate and made a mental note to not pose this question to any more nuns. (And what was a nun doing in a bar anyway...?)

5. "A woman needs someone who will nurture her soul along with all the other things men and women do for each other. But a man who can nurture a soul is probably not going to be able to squish a kitchen bug."

6. "When they are emotional, men cannot confide in other men because it shows a weakness. Women, when they are emo-

tional, confide in other women because it shows their strength."

7. "When women get too emotional, men detach. The more emotional a woman becomes, the more detached the man becomes. When a man gets too emotional, we think he's probably gay anyway."

8. "Women mean what they say. Men mean what they do. Men also mean to do what women say they should do, but usually forget, which is why men can't be trusted with anything important."

9. "When women cheat, men NEVER get over it. When men cheat, women are supposed to just forget about it and get on with their lives. So they do. Women are much more practical about this kind of thing than men. Just ask Hillary Clinton."

10. "Women always want something more from their men, whether time or emotion or more listening, or whatever. Men try to look like they have more to give, but this is rarely the case."

11. "Men are empty boxes women put things in."

12. "When he's arguing with his wife, a man usually becomes a child. This leaves the

wife no choice but to fill the vacancy and become the man."

13. "Women reach conclusions, men jump to them."

14. "Women want to settle down sooner rather than later. Men want to settle down as later as possible, if ever, if at all."

15. "Ask a woman about her greatest orgasm and she might have the date written down somewhere. Ask a man and he will say it was the most recent one. Men are PIGS!!" This lady was on her fifth tequila mimosa by that point and her 'date' was hitting on the bartender pretty hard so, she probably has a point...

Hmmm. Okay, so those are all the responses that are fit to print. There were more, as you can imagine, but they did not really add much to the debate. And in some cases I couldn't read my own writing, or the cocktail napkin ripped. But conducting the survey and now reading back all these responses, I have to conclude that men and women look at each other and see such incredible differences that it's lucky we ever get together at all.

When Women Say "I Know" vs When Men Say It

What a conundrum. The exact same words. The exact same sentence structure. The subject and predicate in exactly the same place. Yet when used by women and men, this tiny little sentence means something completely different.

When women say, "I know," it signals the end of the discussion that was just taking place. It tells the man that he doesn't need to say anything further, that she's got it, that she understands all aspects of his point of view completely. Nothing more needs to be said. So, what a woman is actually saying when she says "I know" once is, "Yes, thank you! Please stop talking now…"

If the man continues mansplaining whatever the subject is, not realizing that the conversation is over, the woman may respond with "I Know, I know…" When the phrase comes twice like this, in quick succession, she is actually stepping it up and her words now mean, "I get it. I understand. I understood a long time ago so just stop talking before I lose what's left of my mind!!"

If the man still doesn't realize that a rare intellectual victory has taken place, the woman will often put three or more "I know's" right in a row, like rapid fire bursts from a machine gun. This may be accompanied by a slight eye roll, or even sometimes the semblance of a hand wave. At this stage the man should be wrapping it up, but sadly, he rarely does. He misses the cue. He flies his paper-airplane-self right off the runway.

So, when she says "I know" three times right in a row, what she actually means is, "ENOUGH ALREADY! JUST SHUT UP AND LET'S MOVE ON FOR CRYING OUT LOUD!!!" In her subconscious mind she might be saying several other things, but in the interest of keeping the relationship alive, she softly and simply adds one last, "I know…" So that's four altogether, which I think basically means "Say one more word and I'm gonna find a new home for this meat cleaver!!!"

Men on the other hand, have a completely different use for these two little words and in using them, are usually trying to express a much simpler message. You will often hear this phrase whenever a man is not quite in his element or has drifted outside his comfort zone. So, for instance, when he's driving and looking for a small street somewhere, the woman with him will say, "I think it's over there," and the man will say, "I know."

Or, when their offspring is upstairs in tears, the woman will say, "I think your daughter needs you right now..." and the man will say, "I know, I know..."

So, when men say, "I know," what they are actually saying is, "I *don't* know." When used twice in a row, "I know I know..." usually means "I *really* don't know..." Three or more times in a row, like bang-bang-bang conveys a feeling of complete desperation and what the man is saying at this point is something like, "I should have listened to my mother and gone to law school...."

Sometimes the use of this phrase is one way men subtly acknowledge that they have no further ideas to contribute to whatever the topic might be or they simply don't remember what the topic was because Sportscenter just started. In many cases "I know" is actually a perfect substitute for "Huh?"

For men, "I know" or one of its derivatives is also one of those chameleon-like phrases that can represent any number of things that are difficult to say. As discussed earlier, we are not above telling the tiniest little fib when absolutely necessary. So instead of saying, "You're right about that," men will say, "I knew that." Instead of saying, "You know what... We might be lost," men will say, "You know what...

I know exactly where we are!" Instead of saying "I'm confused about this," men will say, "I know all about this... I read an article online...."

But honestly, what else can we say? How can we be completely in charge and full of hubris and confidence if we don't appear to know EVERYTHING? It's all part of our mancharade... (Yes, this is a brand new word! Just made it up. Right here at my computer watching the Women's Ping Pong Championships.) Anyway, our mancharade is this: When we know little or next to nothing or actually nothing about a subject, we simply pretend to know it all. It is our way of sharing with the world a little more of our special magic. Some might call it lying, but we just call it "Thriving with Ignorance!"

There are other simple phrases that have completely different meanings when spoken by men or women. A woman says, "I'm Fine. Really, I'm fine." This phrase often means "Later on tonight we're going to fight about that stupid thing you just said." When men say "I'm fine," it means "I'm thinking."

When preparing for an evening out, a woman says, "Can you give me a minute?" and this usually means she needs another hour or so to finish getting ready, and that she doesn't enjoy being rushed through the beautification process. When a man says "Can you give me a minute, it usually means, "I'm thinking..."

A woman says, "Didn't we talk about this?" It most often and most probably means, "Did you forget to pick up... a) dinner; b) the dry cleaning; c) the kids; or d) my mother at the hair place?" But when a man says, "Did we talk about this, or didn't we?" It means, more often than not, "I'm not sure what's happening right now and I'm still thinking."

Women Like Numbers, Men Wish They Didn't

Age. Height. Weight. Measurements. Shoe size. Credit card debt. Number of previous boyfriends/ lovers. Prescriptions. Surgeries. Whatever... The very last thing any man needs to know about any woman he's in love with or in like with or maybe feeling a little something brewing with, are her numerical details. Do not share ANYTHING with us that involves digits. Just nothing. It doesn't add up for us, it adds down! And what's wrong with a little mystery? (Or a lot of mystery actually...)

TMI!! Too much information is the guideline here. Anything related to age is too much information. Age is a landmine. Before you tell us how old you are, ask yourself "What good will it do? What noble purpose will it serve? What will be better if we know you're 50 and not 42? Or 40 and not 36? Or 30 and not 24?" Answer: Nothing. Nothing will be better if a man knows your real age. Nothing at all. In fact, one of the great mysteries will be solved and as you are hopefully coming to realize, the more mysteries the better when you entertain a fourteen-year-old.

Men lock into numbers. We cannot escape them. We hear them and live within their restrictions. We are bound and hounded by them. Fourteen-year-old boys, remember? We are fascinated by what numbers represent, whether statistics for a sports team or the value of our 401k. Numbers, numbers, numbers. We judge ourselves and our friends based on them. They represent much more than just an amount of something. They measure success and failure in a very concise way. The biggest, baddest, highest, lowest, fattest, most attended, best-selling THING, whatever it is, is all based on its numbers. Don't tell us anything we don't *need* to know.

I don't know how old my beautiful wife is and I don't want to know. I don't know how old my ex-wife is either. Sure, I could find out. That would be easy. There's this thing called the internet on most computers now. But that would be too easy and so what? What will be better if I know that detail? Nothing! You know how television adds 10 pounds? Well, tell a man how old you really are, and he will add ten years. Not sure exactly why but I think it happens because maybe he compares that number to how old he is, or how old his mother is, or how long he's owned a certain pair of socks. Or some other thing that's completely irrelevant but will, from that moment on, always serve to remind him how old you are. ("Gosh... My wife is almost as old as these David Bowie albums...") Knowing that might happen, why even bring it up? It does not make us love you more or desire you more. It doesn't make us anything "more" except to be more informed. And that's usually not a good thing.

The same is true regarding your weight. We don't need to know it. No information is better than any information. You say 120. We hear 140. You say 150. We hear 175. You say 200, we hear 300. But that's only because we're not great with personal math. Whatever number you say, we hear at least twenty, thirty or fifty more. And once that number gets in, it sticks. Once heard, never unheard. Once known, never unknown.

The other thing that will really get us all fritzed up and ready to start pulling out our hair is any news or updates regarding your previous romantic entanglements. If you want to send your man around the bend, and maybe even further, start to reminisce about Gerald or Juan or WhoeverItWas from long long ago. Try it and watch your man look for a box to crawl into and spend the next few hours sulking in it. Then, ask yourself why you brought it up anyway. Nothing good will come from this subject. Forget there was ever anyone but the man you're with and he will be quite content with how things are going with you.

My father wrote a film called THE LADY EVE and tried to make fun of his own great weakness, jealousy, by showing what happens to an otherwise normal guy when his new wife starts telling him about all the previous boys. Very funny on film but not at all in real life.

So let's recap. If it's a number, keep it to yourself. Don't mention how you still look good for your age, or how other women your age look much worse. Same with your weight. We just don't need to know. Way the same with romances. And how much money you owe. And your rent payment. And how many years you were in the mental institution. Why remind us? Keep it under wraps for god's sake. Go ahead and celebrate your birthdays, or how much weight you lost or the high school reunion you're about to attend. But just leave out the important details, okay? No numbers. Ever. At all.

Boys really like *not* knowing some things.

Women Remember What They Wore, Men Don't Even Remember What Year

Another big tree in our forest of differences is the way men and women remember important events, data and dates in our lives. First date with you, last date with whomever came before you, the night you got engaged, whatever. Try as men might, there is no point pretending we actually remember unless we have a chance to study up. Why? Cause these kinds of details get conflated with all the other details in our lives and then mulched into a category we call, "Oh yeah. I kinda remember that…"

The backbone of many of our memories is sports and money. So we might remember everything else that happened around that time only as an accompaniment to the sports and money memories of that same time. If our favorite team won an NBA Championship that year, we will definitely remember taking you to Barbados. If we sold a great stock and made a ton on it, then that was the year we got you the nice watch. And so forth. The big sports and money moments are like the Christmas tree, and whatever else happened that year is the ornaments and tinsel. That's a lot of men anyway.

Women kinda remember EVERYTHING that has happened in their lives. And I mean every single detail. The date, time, place, the witnesses, where they were in their lives vis a vis romances, what car they were driving, their favorite actress at the time, the #1 single that week…all of it. Proof that they can remember their lives in incredible detail is best evidenced by the fact that they actually remember what clothes they had on. Like that matters? Like there's any significance whatsoever? They recall that it was the rose-colored suit they wore some night long ago and not the black pencil skirt? What? REALLY? How do they even have enough synapses and neurons to remember that kind of stuff, but more importantly, why? What's the difference and what difference would it make anyway?

I would bet that a large percentage of people who claim to have photographic memories are women, because I just can't see men, most men anyway, trying that on. Our minds don't hold on to the details like that, especially after college and the swilling our brains endured in the decade immediately following.

And even more especially because who really cares if we were wearing the green dive bar t-shirt or the red golf one, the khakis or the shorts. There may have been more important details to commit to memory at the time, such as Brett Favre's completion percentage in a big MNF game or Clayton Kershaw's strikeout totals in a particular season. Or the hole-in-one at Rancho #3. I mean, *these* are important things!

So please don't get mad if we don't remember things. At least not at the granular level that women do. It's not personal. It's just us. It's one more example of the depth and breadth of the gulf that exists between men and women. Women remember almost everything that happened, and men have a fuzzy idea that something definitely happened.

PART 3

Men and Women Getting Together

Sooner or later men do grow up. A little. Actually, as little as possible. But we do grow up. A tiny bit. Just enough for someone to want to consider partnering with us. Maybe to start a romance, have a relationship, raise a family. Serious stuff in other words. We don't change well, but we do come to realize that without a shred of maturity creeping in we might never get to know love and all those other those beautiful things that could take place in our lives.

So Pinky, if you're pondering what I'm pondering, here follow some ideas to think about, and more secrets revealed. These are guidelines to consider and guard rails to avoid should it be the case that magic is in the air and the fourteen-year-old boy in your life is starting to look to his future.

Men Fall in Love with a Face First, Everything Else After

As mentioned earlier, and probably too often, men are simple creatures. Readily understood. Straightforward. Easily given to follow shiny objects and good music and beauty whenever and wherever we find it. And nowhere is this more obvious than when we find the right face, and all the fellas will know exactly what I mean by this.

You can call us shallow. And without depth. And always reaching for something to which we should not even dream of attaining, and that is all true. It is certainly who and what we are. But the truth is, if we are single and see a beautiful face across a restaurant or a street or a casino, we can literally get lost in it. We have to get closer and closer and see if it's for real. We're like bees confronted with an almost perfect flower. We stare. We get googly eyes. We excuse ourselves from whatever we are doing and are practically willing to commit to a brand new life just so long as that face is a part of it. And if we are lucky enough to convince the owner of said face to talk to us, or let us take her to dinner, or to a weekend away somewhere, or someday even marry us, then wow, what a future it might be. My friend Robert was having a drink on his deck late one afternoon and saw "the face" across the shared deck at his next-door neighbor's party. He recalled later that he was dumbstruck when he saw her, from twenty feet away, having a chat with some guy. Even though he had other things to do that night, he changed his plans, dolled up and went next door to the party. Within ten minutes he had found her, introduced himself, made her laugh a couple of times and figured out all he needed to figure out. They were engaged within the year and had one of those destination weddings in Hawaii. Still together, with twin girls who both just got into UC Berkely, they are the perfect example of how this metric works. The right face is all a boy needs to see. If we do not see a future in those eyes and that smile, there is nothing for us there. And we move on.

It's not the hands or the walk or the bum or the boobs or the voice or whatever else is on the list of things men look out for. Sure, these elements matter, but not like the face. It is *a* particular face that a particular man hopes to see looking back at him for the next few months or years or the rest of his life. Or for however long he can keep the dream of love alive in that particular person's heart. Is it immature?

Sure! Is it childish? Yes, of course. But let's not forget what we're really discussing here. The fate of little boys pretending to grow up while fighting like hell to stay forever young. So really, it is just the facts of life to us.

There are a few notable exceptions to this rule. Like arranged marriages, polygamy, and the extraordinarily stupid practice of polyandry – this insanity is when a woman marries a man AND has to sleep with all his brothers too. All of them. (Uhmmm, wtf...?) The vast majority of the rest of us seek and find That Face. We know somehow that it will make all the difference in our lives. We see it and let our hearts fall where they may. This is not a recent phenomenon either. It has been happening from the very beginning and simply continues unabated into the present day.

The English poet Christopher Marlowe wrote several poems and such that sum up a man's whole dilemma in a few pen strokes, including this: "Whoever loved that loved not at first sight?" He also went on and on about Helen of Troy, a mainstay of Greek mythology, who was invented to be held up as one of the most beautiful women in the world. She must have had one of "those" faces. He wrote: "Was this the face that launched a thousand ships?"

Myth or no myth, she must have been some beauty, Miss Helen of Troy. Imagined or Real,

Unimaginable, or just Perfection. Soldiers went off to war for her. Grown men were described as willing to lose their lives for the feeling that they got just *looking* at her.

Shakespeare threw down the same idea with this gem from Romeo & Juliet: "See how she leans her cheek upon her hand. Oh, that I were a glove upon that hand that I might touch that cheek!"

You hear the same idea expressed in a thousand popular songs too but none more so than "Just One Look" or "That Face," or "The Way You Look Tonight" by Frank Sinatra. Both Billy Joel and Bruno Mars had hits with the identically titled tunes "Just the Way You Are." The Beatles said as much with "I've Just Seen A Face" from Rubber Soul. James Blunt added weight to the argument with his mega-hit "You're Beautiful." All this to say, we're all about the face.

I've seen this phenomenon up close and personal, in action, on more than several occasions. The most memorable was one night at an ASCAP Awards dinner. I happened to be sitting next to Stevie Wonder. The guy with him had to run off somewhere and asked me to look after him for a few ticks. So, for a few minutes it was just the two of us, me and Stevie Wonder. Just the two of us, the only people at our own table, in a ballroom with thousands of songwriters and publishers and artists all around us. But for whatever reason, seeing just the two men sitting there, and him that accessible, one by one, women started coming up and asking me to take a picture of them with Stevie. I leaned over and asked him if that would be okay. He whispered back, "Sure, but just tell me what they look like first." As the line formed, I described all the women as if they were finalists in beauty contests, and snapped photo after photo. Finally, he said, "Man, they all can't be *that* beautiful." And I replied, "Stevie, around you they are!" He laughed and we kept it up until his man came back from little boys' room and chased the rest of the line away.

I was thinking then what I'm thinking now: ARE YOU KIDDING ME?!? Here is a *blind* man. He couldn't even *see* their faces, but all he wanted to know was what they *looked* like. He wanted to know if they were beautiful. As all men do, I think. It's just how the cookie rolls or crumbles or however that cliché goes. But it's unbelievable, right? One of the women still has the photo posted on her FB page. (Hey Donna – Here's your shout out, just like I promised…).

So that's it folks. That's what the truth sounds like. Men are all about the face first and don't ever forget it. Even blind men. You can think we are shallow or immature, but that's not how it is and that's not how we see it. In a woman's face, a man sees everything. Whether it is innocence, or commitment, or loss, or the reminder of another face from many years before. In a woman's face a man sees his future, the life he wants to lead, and the love he hopes to have. And if he has any game at all, he convinces the owner of that beautiful face to take a chance on him.

While men will say or do almost anything to make the woman behind that face feel the same way about them, we know it can never be. We know it never will be. No man believes that a woman can feel the same love and depth and truth and hunger that he does. How could she feel everything he feels? It's not possible. All he has to do is look in the mirror to see why. All he sees is *his* face when he looks there, and he knows that his face has none of the beauty and grace that he sees in hers. Men's faces don't have beauty, they have distinction. Men's faces don't have grace, they have character. As men age, our noses actually get bigger! And start to develop pores the size of sinkholes. Our eyes suddenly start to look like they're holding back curtains. Our hairlines disappear and begin to mock us. We get hairs growing out of our cheeks that start to function like feelers. Pretty soon we don't even need to look in the mirror anymore, a glance will do. We know what we're going to see…

So, if there's a man in your life who absolutely loves the way you look, just accept his many compliments. Over and over he will tell you how beautiful you are. And he means it. And you just be gracious about it. Don't tell him you look like hell. Don't tell him why you're not as beautiful as you used to be. Never mention a new wrinkle or a nasty pimple. Just don't. Accept that he finds you beautiful and celebrate that fact every day. Let him love you and your face without compromises or excuses. You won him over *before* hello. It was your face that pulled him into your life in the first place, and it is that same beautiful face that keeps him there, more and more every day.

You're welcome.

Men Love a Face, Women Love a Type

All of us, men and women, are addicted to our passions and our dreams. We live to fulfill them both a little bit every day. And while men reach out for that golden ring every time they see another perfect face, women, as you might expect, handle it a little differently. Because everything is different.

Women like a 'type' of guy and are attracted to the man or men who come closest to that image. Possibilities are endless of course but would include: Big, dumb and athletic. Nerdy, brilliant and hilarious. Long hair and long fingered with smoldering eyes. Latin, with a slight accent and very strong cologne. Intellectual, bookish, and owns cats. Whatever it is that floats her boat, she will more than likely return to that same dock again and again.

Smart people with lots of initials after their names will probably say this has something to do with the woman's dad, what he looked like and how he acted when she was a kid. I'm not going there because I cannot begin to know what motivates women to do anything. But based on what I've seen happen a thousand times at least, it's a type more than anything else that will get a woman to turn her head and look again.

Women Don't Need Handsome, Just Funny or Rich

As mentioned earlier, women are much more complex and nuanced than men in the way they live their lives and in the way they see the things they see. When they look at a man, they are looking at him as a potential partner, a teammate, a provider, a port in a storm, a place to turn, a caretaker of their hearts, and, if they're feeling practical, as a way to look after themselves and their children and their future.

Women may sometimes find that they like a man's face, but unlike men, they will not let that detail overrule and override all the other factors that will need to be considered before, y'know… things move forward.

It's from a long time ago but take Jackie Kennedy as an example. She married one of the best-looking men in the world, Jack Kennedy, and he turned out to be a faithless womanizer who tried to sleep with all her friends. After he was gone, who came after him? One of the richest men in the world, a Greek shipbuilding magnate named Aristotle Oanassis. Not much to look at, but he had a full wallet and a gracious heart and was willing to share everything he had with her. Their marriage vows included trust funds for both her children and a long list of payoffs if they ever got a divorce, which they never did. She was a widow a second time when he passed away about ten years later. But she found in him what she was looking for, and he found in her what he loved looking *at*. She was astonishingly beautiful and he was a Greek shipbuilder. Both of them got what they came for. This type of arrangement seems to be a template that works over and over. Other examples: Donald Sterling and Viv Stefanini (or whatever her real name was). Anna Nicole Smith and that 97 year old guy. Mel Gibson and Oksana Grogorieva. Rupert Murdoch and Jerri Hall. Rupert Murdoch and whomever. And the show goes on and on.

Clearly women don't need their men to be good looking.

Men understand this and know it really doesn't matter what we look like. We don't have that kind of vanity because we don't need it. In our mind's eye we look just as good as we did when we were in our twenties anyway. But more than that, men don't really care about how they look after a certain point, because how funny and successful and engaging or rich they are is all that really matters. Unattractive men can succeed with women just as easily and just as often as the attractive ones, and in many cases even more so. This is primarily because unattractive men have learned to talk past their faces and win women over with their sense of humor or their bank account. As long as they are not clowns about it, men know if they can get a woman to laugh, or let them pay for everything, they have a chance.

Men with a little life experience and a couple of scars know the face is last on the list to the women they are chasing. Who really cares what a guy looks like when women see right past the face anyway? Men wisely care about the assets and portfolios first, and do everything they can to ensure that theirs is bigger and better than the next guy's is. Men don't need to look good to succeed because it just doesn't matter. Plenty of short, bald, unattractive and overweight guys are strolling around with some lovely women on their arms.

Everybody gets what they want in the end. Men want to gaze on a beautiful face every morning and night, and women don't want to live in a trailer park wondering why they married a good looking loser whose best days were in high school. As usual, women are much more adult-like and practical than men. The diminished importance of the face is just one more example.

In Life and Love, Men Believe in Luck and Fate

No matter what has happened along the way, men carry with them an absolute belief in fate and luck. We hold on to the possibility that things are the way they are for reasons beyond our control and we are quite content to live with the results. We try not to take this to extremes, but we are almost childlike in our reliance on the likelihood that things will absolutely positively work themselves out. Some day. Somehow. Some way. We have been like this for multiple upon multiple generations. Consider all the great explorers and artists and generals and scientists who cast their fate to the wind, having no idea what might happen. Many of whom then succeeded or even thrived at the end of the day. There are ample examples of this childlike naiveté lasting successfully throughout a life-time, with luck and fate guiding and guarding their lives like sailors relying on the North Star.

The story that follows is from my own life and provides an illustration of how I trusted in fate and luck, for the hundredth time at least, and in so doing (and by complete accident) changed so many negatives into so many positives. So much so that I might be the luckiest man of all. When fate called, softly and quietly, in a once in a lifetime situation, I was listening. I heard it and I answered. Somehow, and I can't say how honestly, I had always trusted that things would somehow work out, as they always had before. No matter how difficult the challenges or how far they pushed me to the edge (and I hope I get to write *that* book someday), sooner or later something better arrived. This is the greatest example I know of Fate and Luck providing one man the chance he needed to turn things around. It's the story of how I met my wife…

I was at the beginning stages of a divorce from my first wife. Miserable and sad, wincing at the future and hoping against hope that as my life unraveled another chance would come to me. But the last thing I was looking for was a new relationship. The very last thing. I was still living with my first wife and our two sons, but by this time I was sleeping in the study downstairs while she slept upstairs. It was clearly an untenable situation that spoke of many changes coming very soon in all our lives.

It was Groundhog Day. February 2nd, 2004. A band I had signed years before, Outkast, was enjoying a #1 single with "Hey Ya", Roger Federer was the best tennis player in the world, and George Bush was President. On the way home that night, it started to rain and the wind started to howl. And by the time I got near my house it was a sideways rain blowing across the windshield as the wipers swiped hope-lessly. I pulled into a gas station. Filling up my car, there under a canopy, I noticed a woman walking with one of those red plastic gas cans in her hand. She had no umbrella and was braving the rains with no defenses. As she became a smaller and smaller figure on the muddy street, about 200 feet away I saw her emergency lights blinking weakly through the downpour.

Apparently, she had just run out of gas – within a pitching wedge of the gas station, and the penalty was already terribly severe. She was drenched, alone, and being ignored by the hundreds of cars going by. There I was, dry as could be, watching as she tried to get some of the gas from the little red plastic can into her empty tank. And here comes fate.

I was already a few minutes late for dinner but could not leave someone so helpless in a situation so miserable. I pulled out of the gas station and went back the way I came, and made a U-turn, pulling my car up behind hers. I tried to help her but the red plastic nozzle did not fit her car, and gas was spilling all over both of us and all over the wet street. I sug-gested that she get in my car and let me drive her to the gas station. She hesitated but said okay and we drove those two hundred feet, alone together for the first time.

I called AAA and asked them to send a truck for her, with lots of gas in it, and I bought her a cup of coffee and gave her one of my dry golf jackets, and a hat to keep her head warm. I gave her my business card so she could return my gear when she dried out. I went home and did not give the whole thing much more thought. So that was fate, and along came luck.

A few days later I got a box of cookies as a thank you. All it said was "Thank you" with a Mrs. Fields logo on the bottom of the card. I thought to myself, "How about that....I rescued Mrs. Fields!" But a few days after she stopped by my office to return the jacket and hat and say thank you in person. The woman who I met in the lobby that day looked nothing like the drowned and soaking wet figure I had helped in the rain. In fact she was pretty beautiful and I almost got tongue tied, which would have been a real rarity. But thank goodness I didn't. After about twenty minutes of chit chat she clapped her hands on her knees and said, "Well I guess that's it…" and got up to leave.

Out of nowhere I said, "A lot of things had to happen for us to meet the other day. The rain, the gas, the place and time…both of us on that street at that exact moment in time… Possibly we're supposed to know each other." She looked at me differently and asked me what I was asking? I said maybe we go see some music together or have dinner or something simple like that, just be friends. I added that I had two sons who were more important to me than anything in the world, and that I was separated from my wife. She said, "I'm also separated…" Aha! I got a smile on my face and said, "See there, maybe we *are* supposed to know each other…" A week later we saw Elijah Blue at the Troubadour, and had dinner next door at Dan Tana's. My dearest friend Michael Rosen stopped by our table to assess and approve. He quietly gave me a big thumbs up. And then she and I started seeing each other more and more, again and again.

We have been together ever since, without even a day's interruption. Our son was born May 5th, 2009, and we were married January 10th, 2010. We have never had a fight, or even an argument really. She is my peace, she is my light, she is my everything. I'm so thankful we found each other.

She was the last thing I was looking for, the last thing I ever expected to find, and despite that, the little boy in me was willing and open to the possibility that fate would come tumbling into his life. Fate put one of the great loves I will ever know right in front of me, in the person of a lady in the rain. Luck ran alongside – and made sure I said the right thing at the right time.

For most men, fate and luck are as reliable as air and water. They get us through tough times and great difficulties. They see us through the bad days. They are the hidden assets we come to rely on because so many of our well thought out plans keep falling through.

If women were more aware of men's reliance on these completely intangible forces in our lives, they might let it work to *their* advantage. Women could see more than the childlike (and probably idiotic) look on a man's face when he is struggling to say something brilliant about getting together with you. Women might see past the awkward hemming and hawing when a man approaches, hoping to find the words that will win you over in a sentence or two. Women would see beyond the likely uncomfortable situation she's in, possibly with a complete stranger, who might be hoping his future and his destiny is you.

Maybe just maybe meeting you is the stroke of luck and twist of fate he has been waiting for his whole life. If you let him in, he just might start to believe that his forever has finally begun.

While Men Fall in Love, Women Consider the Possibilities

In addition to everything else we do completely differently, it's the actual instant of falling in love with one another that also really sets men and women apart. Maybe when we are very young it's more similar, everyone's willing to take more risks and so forth, but once women start to grow up (and men pretend to start to grow up) you can really see the separation in the methods. Ultimately it becomes two completely different solutions to the same problem. You can look at this dichotomy as one more example of what a miracle it is that we get together at all.

When they are young, women might let themselves get swept off their feet, now and again. Maybe they're attending a great party or dancing and drinking into the wee hours at some club. The key term is that they "let themselves." They are basically in control of the situation because, for the most part, women are asked to do things and have the choice to say yes or no. But then somewhere along the journey to adulthood and beyond, a more practical side emerges. The realization starts to dawn on them that the "fall" in "falling in love" might be like the "fall" in "falling down some stairs." There could be injuries and ligament damage and a lot to be embarrassed about. And then of course they have to walk back up that same flight of stairs and start the whole process all over again. This will get pretty tiresome after a while, so they stop the "love at first sight" thing, and advance to a "more careful consideration" program. I *think* this is what happens, but obviously on account of my gender and my age and so forth I really don't know all that much about women, even now. Clearly. It's just a bunch of guesses on my part. I'm like a deaf guy playing a trumpet. I feel the vibrations, but I can't hear a thing.

Since men are basically fourteen-years-old on the inside, and fight getting older like Sugar Ray Leonard fought Thomas Hearns, men get swept off their feet on a constant and regular basis. For men this can happen at the gas station just as easily as it can happen watching a girl in a Netflix movie or sitting with someone on a first date. We don't need the lighting to be perfect. We don't need a strolling violinist. We don't care. We *want* to be in love. Yes, that's what I said. We want that rush, and the electric feeling that ensnares us in its stunning web. Practical considerations are swept away like peanut shells at a ballpark. We just want it to happen, and if possible, again and again.

Guests at weddings are a good example of this very different metric. Single women go to weddings to witness another member of the sisterhood moving forward in her life, taking up the responsibilities of wife and possibly family, committing to a bold future, and all the other milestones (and millstones) that she hopes to achieve herself someday. Men go to show support and offer their unspoken sympathies to the groom. A single women might compare herself to the bride and measure her steps against those of the woman she sees walking down the aisle. Men wonder if there will be any cuties at the reception, and if the beer will be cold. A single woman might think that maybe, just maybe, she will meet someone special today, cause it's a wedding and love is in the air and all that stuff. Men go to weddings with the same mind set they use to go to a bar or a party or anywhere else: have some fun, maybe have a little too much to drink, possibly discuss whatever championship is currently being decided, and try to get home safely with a couple of phone numbers.

Somewhere between the two extremes men and women have to start compromising if they want to get with each other. Hopefully it's near-ish to halfway, understanding that both sides are very suspicious of the other on the one hand, but very intrigued on the other. By the time the woman has decided that she might be able to fall in love with any particular man, he may have already figured out that she's perfect for him and everything he's been looking for all these years. She took weeks and it took him five minutes. In this case it's her responsibility not to scare him off with too much adult conversation and a recounting of the woes of her last few relationships. (This kind of thing is covered in "So You Found Someone New, Now What?" coming up in just a few pages!) She should approach him like she would any wild animal. Use a kind soft voice, make no sudden moves, and offer some treats. This usually works well.

Men and women fall in love for completely different reasons. Women, once they've grown up, fall in love as a way of advancing their lives and circumstances, moving ever closer to their dreams, whatever those may be. Men fall in love because they can't help it. It just feels so good. Women fall in love as a way to get started on that all important "next chapter" in their lives.

Men fall in love by accident, sometimes multiple times a day. One approach is very much cognitive, the other is very primitive. One is intellectual, the other is instinctive. But you know what? Both work and they will just have to suffice until someone comes up with a better solution.

This is not to say that women are not romantic, or not willing to throw themselves in front of a
moving train to prove they love a man. Or cut off
an ear. Maybe some do. But that's not how it usually
works. In many cases, a man with some money and
a sense of humor might be a lot of what a woman is
hoping to find, provided he's not an asshole. A man's
wealth, as long as there is some, can be the permission slip a woman needs to move forward with a
particular relationship. As it should be! Why would
or should a woman share her treasures with someone
who has no treasure himself? Especially since we've
established that the man is more than likely a fourteen-year-old on the inside who's just pretending to
know what he's doing anyway.

There are some instances where a woman might
choose poverty over love, but those situations are
rare. Like the Alabama prison guard who recently
helped her new man, a murderer on death row (!!),
escape his life sentence – one week before she was
set to retire with a $75K yearly pension! Talk about
a bad choice! These two birdbrained lovebirds drove
around for a few days before she realized the enormity of the mistake she'd made. He survived the
man- hunt and got sent back to prison. She did not
even make it home. Where was her practical femi-
nine nature when she needed it most? Why wasn't
she considering some of the possibilities? Okay

maybe she's the outlier. But people like her exist. Sorry to report but they sometimes marry their high school sweetheart and let him move in with her and her mother. Yikes.

The word must have gotten out to the world that women are often looking for someone with a little wealth and a modicum of a sense of humor. Some men have figured this out and have designed ways to separate these women from their fortunes, whether large or small. The worst example is the Tinder Swindler. Somehow this guy got so many women to believe he was something he was not they made a Netflix series about him.

Even though they were somewhat suspicious about his intentions and apparent wealth, the Tinder Swindler was able to convince thirty or so women that he was rich (which he wasn't) and then convinced those same women to give him their life savings to help him stay rich. How did he do it? He preyed on them, like a fox after a chicken. He knew what they wanted (a rich-ish guy) and made sure he played the part. All he needed to do he did on the first couple of dates, at least that was what his victims recounted to the authorities.

He made sure that he looked very wealthy. He would pick them up in a limousine (rented from a cousin) and take them to an expensive dinner (at a restaurant where another cousin tended bar). He would complain about rich people problems (the price of a Rolex, etc) and then show them photos of himself sitting in his private plane (another cousin worked at an executive airport). And that was all most of the women he shafted (haha) needed to hear and see. One after another, women were tantalized by the possibilities.

With his hooks in their hides, the Tinder Swindler would start to work them into the idea that a life with him was possible, if he could just get through his present difficulties. Such as? His enemies were after him. His diamond mine needed a new drill. His private jet needed the seats reupholstered. His blank needed a blank. Etcetera. And so on. Women got in line to throw their money at him, never to see him or it again. All the women he duped were most likely after the same thing, love. But in the words of my old friend Mickey Gilley, they were looking for love in all the wrong places. They were confusing the appearance of cash with the possibility of a romance.

But this sad story reveals a sad truth. Women want their worlds to get better with every romance. They want their next love affair to be an upgrade. They want the next entanglement to help improve things, to make their lives better. And they are often willing to sacrifice a bit of their present to make a bet on a better future. They want to step up, not down or sideways. An apparently rich guy like Tinder Swindler clearly offered better prospects and took full advantage of it. I think it's a rarity. Most of the men I know wouldn't have the gall or gumption to cheat and lie and thieve like that. Most of the men I know would have been honored just to be in a relationship that worked and made everyone in it happy.

Suffice to say that falling in love is very serious business for both men and women, and the different approaches to letting love happen vs. making love happen underscore how incredibly lucky we are to have gotten this far as a species in the first place.

If He Wants You, You'll Know.
If He Doesn't, You'll Really Know

Men hide in plain sight. Sure, there's a little trick-
ery now and again, and maybe a lie or two just to
get through a day, but otherwise, as I've mentioned
here several times now, what you see is what you get.
We're clear as crystal for the most part, if anyone
cares or wants to notice.

Nowhere is this more true than when one of us
wants to be with one of you. We really couldn't be more
obvious about it. That's because we are so obvious with
our intentions and desires about everything. If we're
after someone, they better know it! The way we look
changes. The way we talk changes. We might even start
to dress a little better and consider getting a haircut. We
bathe more often, stand up straighter, floss the choppers
whether they need it or not. We are very attentive to
details that we might have otherwise overlooked. This
is because we want to be seen and noticed by one of
you. We want to be observed. We want you to see us
and then like what you see. And if we're good enough

at hiding our foibles and putting forward our best sides, we may just have a chance to be with one of you.

Ah yes. But the opposite tack is also just as apparent. If we're not interested in one of you, we couldn't make it any clearer. Our intentions are so very striking. It's like a roadmap printed in invisible ink: there's nowhere to go. We don't care if you're on time or if you're late. We don't care if you show up or don't. We don't care if you look cute or not. We don't notice the new shoes or the frosty tips in your hair. We could care less if you're having drinks with another dude at this point, and that's really big. None of that means a thing to us because we don't give a hoot one way or another. That's the proof we're not interested in you in the slightest.

If that's the state of the situation, it means there is no situation. And maybe you should look elsewhere 'cause here there's nothing here to see. No matter how many suggestions you make or daring chances you take, or sexy dresses you adorn yourself in, and regardless of the subliminal messages you try to send, or the perfume you wear, it all means absolutely nothing.

It's like going to an art museum with Steve Wynn. It's just not gonna matter.

Save yourself time and heartache. Look for a man who's looking for you.

Women Marry Men They Hope to Change, Men Hope the Women They Marry Never Change

When a woman falls in love with a man, she often falls in love with all the *potential* of that man too. She doesn't just see who he is, she sees all he could be. She does not fall for what he is, she falls for what he *will* be, as though the man she met was just the rough sketch, and not the actual piece of art. She looks into his murky future and sees what kind of guy she hopes he *might* be someday. Or she has a pre-set ideal and finds the man who is closest to that ideal, her hope being to make him undergo the changes necessary to *become* that ideal. She might be thinking, I'll get him to stop drinking so much, I'll get him to spend less time with his college friends, I'll make him dress better and start acting like a man instead of a child… and so on.

Well, I got some news for you – those of you who look at men that way. If he's drinking and chilling with his pals and acting like a child all the time, *that might be who he really is.* Maybe that's how he turned out. Maybe the turkey came out of the oven like that – a little undercooked! Maybe he is a done deal and you have to find someone who's got more to offer and less for you to try to change about him.

Frogs rarely turn into princes, no matter how many times you kiss 'em.

For the woman who does not recognize that we don't change well, she sees the road ahead much differently than the man she's picked. She pushes him to give her more, in new and different ways, in ways that he has never given to anyone before or hasn't given to anyone in a long time. She might ask him to be more sensitive, and to listen better, and to show that he cares about her and her life, and less about him and his. She might want him to spend more time at home, and less with his pals, and be nicer to her friends, and more selective with his. The net effect of all the changes is that there will be less "him" at the end of the day. And though she hopes that all the transformations will bring the two of them closer, sorry to say but it's unlikely. He might grow up a little, but it's not who he really is anymore. He will be more lost than he ever was. He'll look in the mirror and see a stranger. It will be like Tarzan looking at himself in a seersucker suit.

The problem here is clear. Most men believe they are fine just the way they are. We feel that we are, like Mary Poppins opined, practically perfect in every way. We feel this way for good reason. Our mothers have been telling us the same thing every day of our lives. And, we always believe our mothers. So, if a girlfriend or fiancé or wife starts to suggest some changes, regardless of how well-intentioned those may be, we balk. Like circus donkeys at quittin' time. And there are plenty of good reasons why. We don't know *how* to be anyone else! We're thrilled just to be here pretending to be *this* person! Esctatic every day just being this guy! We can hardly believe we've pulled off the ruse this long anyway. We can't go changing anything now!

It took us all these years to get here, and get everything about ourselves pretty much just right, so to us we're a finished product. This *is* us. As far as we are concerned, the cookies have been taken out of the microwave and they are not going back in. By the time we start meeting pretty girls and trying to get them to take their clothes off, we have become pretty good at the charade. We are quite content being who we pretend to be. We are by now pretty certain of our style and panache. Maybe there are a few imperfections, but these are completely outweighed by our many *per*fections. We love being us. We don't want anything to be different. And this is why our dreams are much simpler than most of our partners. We're living the dream already. This is why we don't need any more than our three emotions. (Remember? Happy, Sad, and Angry.) Same with someone's continuing evaluations of us or well-intentioned suggestions either. Not gonna happen, not easily anyway. We're closed! This is it! When it comes to romance and relationships, the deal is done. We just want to be with someone who loves us *for* us and *as* us and wants to let us *be* us.

To operate successfully as men, it is essential that the women in our lives accept us for who we are. As if this guideline has been chiseled in granite and placed at the base of Mt. Rushmore. We are who we are. It's a fact of our lives. If we can find a woman who accepts this as a fact of her life too, then all's good. Her acceptance of us, as us, is a big part of our ultimate happiness being on this earth. A few minor improvements are possible, yes, but even fewer are welcome. This is how things turned out. This is who we were meant to be. As Popeye so perfectly put it to Olive Oyle, "I yams what I yams."

Men are like great books. It's up to the reader to figure out what's great about them. It's not up to the book. The book is done.

To understand this whole concept, you must understand that, generally speaking, men love sameness. We wear the same clothes and the same styles, over and over, until forever sets in. We like to eat in the same restaurants, over and over, for years and years. We identified a hair style in our early teens and have stayed with it pretty much until the present day, or until we finally throw in the proverbial towel and allow ourselves to get bald. Same everything is just fine with us. Especially when it comes to the key elements of who and what we are, how we dress and how we act, and how those details might impact a romantic relationship.

Please remember that we are here, but not here. We're not really adults. At all! We're just pretending to be adults. We're bluffing our way along and, if there's a problem, bluffing some more. Hoping no one ever figures it out. Open any man and you will see the boy inside him jerking levers and hitting switches and laughing at all the trouble he's causing or giggling about all the relationships he's having. We are puppeteers, pulling strings and saying things, watching ourselves act out the role of "man," but knowing that in many ways it is only a part we play.

Now on to the other side of the street. For a man, the woman he falls in love with is the woman he wants to be with and stay with. From now until the foreseeable future comes to an end. Not a radically different her. Her, the same knockout he met and fell in love with in the first place. Same hair, same eyes, same lips, same everything. As Billy Joel mentioned, we love you just the way you are. Full Stop. End of Story. So, what does this mean? What is the practical impact? It's this. *Men don't want anything to change.* We need everyone to stick as closely as they possibly can to the original specs in every way, whether style or image or way of living. Especially the way you look. Change a little on the inside if you absolutely have to, but please leave the outside alone. You don't add extra wide tires to a Ferrari! You don't switch up the hands on a Rolex to look like Mickey Mouse hands! And you can't go from redhead to blonde-head in one crazy visit to the hair salon and expect the man you're with to go along with it. He might say it's fine but, on the inside, he's screaming out words that rhyme with FIRETRUCK!!! C'mon!! We hate change. We don't change well, and we don't want you to change either. Stick with the thing that worked so well in the first place. Men ultimately love women for many reasons, but one of them is absolutely the way they look. I know it sounds petty but the truth hurts. Sorry. Get too far away from the look of the person your man fell in love with in the first place and it totally upsets the order and balance of our juvenile universe. What we like to call the Time-Space Continuum. We like things the way they are because the way they are is the way they are supposed to be. Isn't that right?

It's kinda childish but it makes perfect sense to us.

Men Need Sex to Feel Loved, Women Need Love to Have Sex

So many relationships are doomed, over before they even begin. Neither side really understands what the other side wants or is even looking for, and nobody dares to even bother to ask. Men push awfully hard to get a woman into a bed and women push back just as hard to make sure the guy has "feelings" before they get there.

Women think that the more time they are being chased the more time the guy will have to fall in love with them. Guys just don't see it that way. For most of us, the chase is a waste. It's a waste of time, money, energy and effort. A long time spent chasing a woman simply indicates to the man what he fears most anyway: that he has no game.

Composer and conductor, icon and maestro Duke Ellington had a great solution to this problem. He only spent time with women who wanted to spend time with him. It made his life so much simpler. He never chased anyone, but he was always with someone. Not all of them were beautiful. Not all of them were supermodels. Not all of them were worth a second look. But they all wanted to be with him. So, he obliged them. He was a genius.

For whatever reason, men connect the physicality of making love to the emotionality of being *in* love. The two are tied to one another in men's minds and hearts like a kite to a string. One without the other makes no sense. Physical love encourages emotional love. Not the other way 'round. If you wish you can consider us shallow or childlike for feeling this way, but at some point you might have to accept that this is just the way it is.

We need to touch with our bodies to feel love with our hearts.

Another point to consider is the timing and sequence of the events. If the lovemaking is delayed for no good reason other than to meet the standards of a religion or culture or the outdated preconditions of someone's parents, there is all the more pressure upon the act, when it finally happens, to be the most magical thing that ever happened and completely worth the long wait. Which probably won't be the case because the first time together for a couple is almost always full of missteps and awkwardness, bumbling and stumbling. Whereas if the man and woman had just gone to bed together in a more natural sequence, their being lovers would happen without all the unnecessary expectations.

At the end of the day, men and women are all looking for the same thing: a great love and a great lover. Solving both mysteries at the same time saves a lot of heartache. If you don't like the man you're with, get with a man you want to be with. It's that simple a solution. Don't worry, there's millions and millions of us. Men are like the Paris Metro. There's another one coming in just a couple of minutes.

And if you're not sure how to meet that man, read on.

How to Meet Any Man

Have you ever been somewhere and happened to see a man you would like to meet or, at the very least, get to know a little better? More than likely he's a perfect stranger of course... Maybe at a party, or a bar, or a reception, you looked across the room and saw someone that caught your eye and might even have taken your breath away? Maybe this was a man standing by the bar talking to a bunch of other men, or a man just standing by himself looking out at the sea. Maybe you liked the color of his eyes, or the way he laughed. Whatever it was about him, there was something that intrigued you and urged you to find out more about him and what he was all about. Well, we men understand. It happens. Not often, enough, but it does happen. And so there you are, thinking to yourself, how do I get something under-way with this handsome so-and-so without giving him the wrong idea and starting the whole thing off on the wrong foot, like that other time...? Easiest thing to do is nothing, but what fun is that?

So, what to do, what to do? You want to meet him but at the same time you want to completely avoid all the usual nonsense, like having to ask a friend if they know him. Or having to ask the host to introduce you. Or having to dilly dally and futz around just to be sure the first moment is something "perfect." And all of that nonsense is likely a perfect waste of time because next thing you know he's in the valet line chatting up some divorcée and your moment of opportunity has passed.

So, I'm here to tell you there's a better way to handle it. Remember from earlier…we fall in love with the face first. Period. End of story. So, the best and smartest thing to do is to get Your Face in front of His Face and see what happens! Let nature and nurture take their course. If he likes what he sees, then game on. If he doesn't like what he sees then game over. Twenty seconds of courage is all you need!

While there are any number of ways to get yourself and your face noticed, *the best way is a good question.* Ask him a question that requires him to look at your face before answering, and his answer will tell you almost all you need to know about this particular man and what he's like. Just one question, and you will learn, in so many ways, what he's all about, and whether or not he would be interested in you, and whether or not you should be interested in him. Imagine that. One little question provides all those answers. *If you have the guts to ask it!*

Men have found themselves in this same situation throughout their lives. Starting in second grade, right up to yesterday. We see someone attractive and try to figure out what to say besides, "Uhmmm…" 96.3% of the time it's a complete fiasco. No woman wants to be approached by a complete stranger unless she's a professional or she *loves* tequila. So please let that temper your approach. The man you are about to walk up on has probably experienced the same swirl of emotions and rush of adrenaline that you are feeling more times than Bugs Bunny has said "What's up Doc?" *Meaning this man will be more sympathetic and understanding than you think!* He might actually enjoy it on some level. Anyway, back to you and the man you want to meet…

Work your way through the crowd and find yourself next to the lucky candidate and bump elbows or tap him on the shoulder or whatever it takes to get his attention. When he finally looks at you, and this is the critical moment by the way, you then say, "Excuse me… Have you seen my husband?" That's it. That's the million-dollar question. In the next few seconds, so much will be revealed about him you won't even need to see his I.D. If he's a jerk, he will dismiss your question with a shrug of his shoulders. He might say something callous like, "Lady, how am I supposed to know your husband…I don't even know you." You will know instantly that he's not the man you thought he might have been, that he has no sense of adventure, and thus he's not really worth pursuing. Any responses that are rude or dismissive in any way give you this message: Wrong Guy, Keep Moving. Twenty seconds is all it took. And you are saved the hassle and embarrassment of getting introduced, having an awkward first date, having an awkward phone call or text to say there will be no second date, and so on and so on. No thank you!

But suppose his reaction to your question is more respectful and nuanced, and he is kinda intrigued. Suppose he reveals that he possesses many of the wonderful things you were hoping he would possess. Suppose he cocks his head to one side when he gets both eyes on you, and a funny look comes over his face. And suppose it's the look a man gets when he sees a woman he was hoping he could meet, maybe who he always wanted to meet. And there she is standing right in front of him. Suppose the look on his face says, "Who is this angel before me?" Then he manages to gather himself and say, "No, I haven't seen your husband, but who is the lucky fella?"

In that answer, or one close to it, he reveals that he has a generous and complimentary nature, and that he's quick on his feet and quick with his wits.

And, by the way, that he obviously finds you to be attractive in return. So far so good, right? What happens next is up to you, of course. What happens next is called conversation. And chances are this is a man who might be worth having a conversation *with*. Your next response might be funny and inviting. You might say, "My husband? I don't know. I haven't met him yet." Or something else short and sweet. A quick line that hints at things but doesn't offer anything; a few words to encourage, to say let's keep this going a little. And you're off to the races, without giving up an ounce of your decorum or an inch of your dignity. You have simply and gently invited this man to look at your face. And if he likes what he sees to get to know you better. And what happens after that is completely up to the two of you and the magic of that moment.

At my persistent urging, a friend of mine tried this recently. She spotted what she thought was a unicorn and decided to cut to the chase. Handsome, tall, surrounded by friends, had a nice laugh... everything she liked. So, she found herself next to him somehow and asked, "Have you seen my husband?" He turned, got a good look at her and said, "Why, yes I have! As a matter of fact, I saw him in my bathroom mirror this morning." Aha! Well well well... What a way to begin a love story! She suddenly found herself with a real possibility on her hands. She knew that she might have found some-one who might see in her all that she hoped she saw in him. His funny answer proved that he had some grace and compassion, and a sense of humor. And as it turned out, like most little boys, he trusted com-pletely in fate and luck and had always hoped that the woman that he was supposed to be with *would* appear out of nowhere, like she just did. They're still together by the way. And one of the cart girls at my golf club tried it on one of the members and, even though it's top secret, they are currently dating! Just sayin'…

Something very much like this scenario hap-pened with Prince William and Princess Catherine, the future King and Queen of England. Both were attending St. Andrews University in Scotland. Danny, my Scottish caddy there at the Old Course, who swore on my new putter that he was in the room when it happened, said the two of them met at a small coffee shop on City Road near Tom Morris Drive, in the city of St. Andrews. He told me they practically bumped into each other in the restaurant's small confines, Catherine at one table, William at another. As she got up to leave, *she* said something like, "Maybe *we* can have a coffee sometime…"

Okay, she didn't use my line exactly, but she accomplished the same goal. She got him to look at her face! Work with me here people! The prince had a chuckle and admired her forthrightness and confidence and said as much to his bodyguards.

Princess Catherine wasn't precisely hitting on His Royal Highness, she was just making sure he *noticed* her. And of course, her face. Which is the whole point of this exercise. Let a man get a good look at you and then see what happens. Catherine let him know she was alive, and available, and made sure that he noticed *her*, not just the other way round. The point is that she gave him an easy opening and that was all he needed. That might be all most men need.

Suppose that the husband line is not right for you. Maybe you are too young or not young enough. Whatever. There are plenty of lines or phrases you can use to catch a man off-guard. Let him see you while you see him for all he is. As a for instance, suppose you're at some big party and you see the man you want to meet. You ingeniously find yourself standing right next to him and you say, "Do you know where they keep the Picasso?" As you now know, he will take a look at you and come back with something that reveals all you need to know. If he's brilliant and quick on his feet and possibly the man you've been looking for, he'll get a glimpse of your beautiful face, play along and say, "I've been looking for it all night! Where is it?" If he's dull as hell he might say, "What's a Picasso...?" In which case you start humming "Hit The Road Jack" to yourself, get on your bye-bye bicycle and get the hell out of there. The least painful version of this gambit is to put a gentle hand on the lucky fellow's arm to be sure you have his attention, and say, "Excuse me... Haven't we met?" Whatever his answer is, there's *your* answer. If he loves what he sees, you'll know it. And if he doesn't, you'll know that too. Instantly.

So, in summary of this most important discussion, if or when or whenever you see a man you want to meet, just get his attention. That's all you have to do. Just let him get a good look at your face. He will reveal what he is and who he is. Maybe it's one of the questions I have suggested, or it's Princess Catherine's, or maybe it's one of your own design. Whichever you decide, just have complete faith and ask it. Jerks will be jerks and knights will be knights. But on such short notice, with their guards down, *men cannot help but be themselves.* We *will* reveal our true selves to you. We can't help it. If you like what you see, you let things move forward, and if you don't, that's the end of it right there. Just be courageous! For twenty seconds! Ask him a good question. In the answer you will learn all you need to know about him and the possibility of a future together.

Seven Questions You Just Have to Ask

It might be a first date. It might be a last date. You'll only know for sure once you're in the middle of it and the reveals are revealed. Whatever the case, whatever the circumstance, you will know the person you are talking to much better after they answer these seven questions.

(Over the course of 25+ years in the music business, I interviewed at least a thousand people for various positions, and every one of them had to survive these inquiries. One guy made a portrait of me with these questions serving as the keystone of the painting. I didn't hire him but maybe I should have…)

The questions do not pry, but the answers certainly divulge. And not in an abusive or bullying way, just revealing some simple facts that will add up to provide a version of the sum total of who that person is, what they think about, and how they handle their life. The answers will help you determine if you want them in your life. More importantly, in your love life.

Here are the questions. Best asked in this order, with lots of follow up questions and interjections as well.

1. What is the last book you recommended? (Not *read*, recommended.)
2. What is the last film you recommended? (Not just *seen*...)
3. Is there a philosophy you live your life by?
4. Who is the most important person in your life?
5. Is there a story from your life that shows how you faced a difficult challenge and how you overcame it?
6. You're driving. You come to a yellow light at an intersection. Do you slam on the brakes to stop or do you hit the gas and race through?
7. You have one vote for the greatest song ever written. What song gets your vote?

And there they are. You will learn, in the answers, the how and why and what of that person. Do they read books? Do they know films? Do they listen to music? Do they have an existential understanding of their place in the world and how they fit? Do they have a grand enough view of their lives to employ and enjoy a philosophy while they are living it?

But it's not only the answers that you are looking for. It's the person's persona *while* they answer. Do they hide themselves in their replies or just come right out and say what's really on their mind. Watch closely, for instance, as they try to come up with the greatest song ever written. You will see them truly at a loss, simply because the question is so huge and so personal all at the same time. I have seen people look at me as if to say, "How could you ask me that?" and then take five minutes before deciding they could not decide what the greatest song was.

These questions are so helpful also because they get a conversation going without you having to do any heavy lifting. You don't have to be charming or even engaged. You just ask the questions. Everything you want to know, and maybe some things you don't, will soon be apparent to you. For the most part, the answerer will not even know that you have just learned everything about them that you would ever want to learn.

The seven questions have multiple uses and possibilities that may not be so readily apparent. A friend of mine asked me to have lunch with his daughter and her fiancé. They had just got engaged and my friend didn't think much of his daughter's choice. But he didn't want to interfere, so he asked me to interfere

for him! As the song says, that's what friends are for...
The three of us sat down at a very nice spot and I was
immediately unimpressed by the slightly overweight
guy who didn't eat with his mouth closed. He was 14
years old in so many ways, and in none of the ways
I cared for. He was kinda rude to the daughter, and
pushy about what he wanted to do that day and left
me feeling that my friend was right: Rich Daughter
might have picked a real loser, or so it appeared.

So, I asked the idiot if it would be okay if I asked
him the Seven Questions. He said sure in a conde-
scending way that apparently came quite naturally to
him. As his answers spilled out, they revealed more
than the daughter needed to know about the mess
she was about to be in. His philosophy was "Fake
it till you make it!" His most important person was
his mother (with his fiancé sitting right there next to
him!). And when he said the greatest song ever written was "God Save The Queen" it was like a bomb
dropped. She looked at me in shock and awe. The
marriage was postponed and ultimately forgotten
about and they were no longer a couple in a couple
months. She went and found a great guy who she was
meant to be with and they have three kids. Needless
to say my friend has never stopped thanking me.

All that to say that whatever the reason, these
are seven questions you just have to ask. They reveal
what should be revealed, and hide nothing.

How to Tell A Man Might Be A Good Father

Imagine if you could look around corners and forward into time. Then imagine you could see things that *might* happen and events that might take place there in your future. Where would this be more valuable than in choosing the man you will try to make a life with? Where would this vision be more needed than when you are deciding who would be the best person to have a family and try to raise children with? With just a couple of simple observations, it will be possible to gain a measure of understanding as to what the future might hold. It's not a perfect view but it is a glimpse of what might be waiting for you just ahead.

Obviously, no one can ever know what the future will hold, or what life will do to someone to change what they will be like in the future. But, there are clues. There are hints and suggestions all over the place. How could there not be? You might look at one thing someone does to see what it says about another thing they *might* do. The reflection of one type of action might indicate how that person will act and react in other similar circumstances. I've outlined below some ideas on how to peer into the darkness of the future to help you illuminate what maybe there for you.

It's very difficult for men to hide who they are. Fourteen years old basically. Hopes and dreams pinned to their shirts like a note to show to the teacher. Sure, men can shower and steam, shave, and douse themselves with cologne, but at a certain point the truth reveals itself. As Robert Prosky states so eloquently in the film CHRISTINE, "You can't polish a toid…" Every man thinks he will be a good father, if not a great one. At least that's what most of us tell the girls into whose beds we are trying to climb. But very few of us are really all that sure about our fathering ability and what we will be like. No matter when it happens or how it happens, we are rarely ready to change gears and buy a minivan and get a haircut and suddenly be a dad. It surprises us like we're playing with a Jack-in-the-Box that opens one note too early. But with a little observation and a little prescience, it is not all that difficult to tell which guy is going to be the best dad. Most likely the best dad anyway.

This exercise is in two parts. Observation of the subject in question, and then, a field test to confirm the results. Let's start with the observation. You have to look at three key relationships the man has established, and how he handles these will tell you, most likely, how he'll handle a relationship with a son or daughter.

First, look at the man's relationship *with himself.* How a man treats himself is an indication of how he will treat others in his life, particularly his own kids. For instance, is he nice to himself? Is he kind to himself? Does he like who he turned out to be? Is he generous about the trips and clothes and things he wants to buy for his own happiness? Or does he constantly remind himself of his past mistakes and how they are keeping him down? Is he willing to forgive and forget his blown opportunities (and there will be plenty to think about...)? Or does he handcuff himself with regrets about things he can no longer do anything about? Does he encourage himself to experience new things in new places with new people? Or does he limit his exposure to his life and hibernate rather than have-a-blast? The more kindness he shows to the little boy inside him tells you how much kindness he will show to the little boy or girl who might show up in his life someday. Every answer is another brick in the wall, another stroke of the brush painting the portrait of his life and his fathering. This is all to say that if he loves himself, there's a good chance he can love someone else, particularly a child. And conversely, if he doesn't love himself and who he turned out to be, it will be that much harder for him to let some innocent little person win over his heart someday.

Second, look at his relationship *with waiters.* Yes, I realize this sounds trivial but me and the kid writing this book have knowledge to share on this subject. How a man treats the people who bring him food and drink is one of the clearest indicators yet available of how much that man can respect, appreciate, understand and empathize with the people around him. And it tells anyone who wants to know how that man views the importance of kindness and generosity in his life. Waiters have to put up with almost anyone and everyone who shows up to eat, and it can be a miserable gig if the clientele are selfish and self-absorbed a-holes. The person who treats the waiter poorly reveals themselves to be a self-absorbed a-hole. If a man can't be nice to the waiter, who is busting his/her/their ass just to keep his hopes for a good dinner alive, how will he be nice to a child who is going to spend a lifetime busting his/her/their ass just to keep his heart alive? How a man handles the one is a good indicator of how he will handle the other.

Third, look at a man's relationship *with his mother.* This relationship, more than any other, reveals who that man is now and who he was back then, when his relationship with her was the only thing that mattered in his life. His relationship with his mother tells you many things you will need to know about what sort of father he will be.

Why? Because he will treat his children very much the same way he treats his mother. Both his mother and his child will rely on him much more than he wishes they did. Both child and mother will insist on his time and attention much more than he has available to give. Both mother and child will expect the best of him, always, regardless of how little he has left in the tank.

It requires just as much patience and grace for a man to be kind and forgiving with his mother as it does for him to be kind and forgiving with his children.

Especially as his mother ages. At some point, both his mom and his kids will become very needy, and both will ask him too many questions, and both will be impatient with his answers. Both will spill something or break something valuable, completely by accident of course, not that that matters. Both will want more of his time than he has to give. At some point a mother will rely on her son in the same way that he, the baby, relied on her. This is the nature of the relationship that develops and matures over the years between them. If he just "puts up" with his mother, he will more than likely just "put up" with his kids.

So, look to see... Is he kind and thoughtful with his mother? Is he forgiving of her, her hesitations and missteps? Does he listen to her questions all the way through, or does he cut her off? Does he anticipate her needs and wants? Is he embarrassed by her getting older right before his eyes? Watch him with his mom and it will reveal many elements of his nature. His reactions to her and the way he treats her will tell you how he will likely react to his children. And this will give you insight on whether he will be a good father. Or not. The kind of son a man is paints the portrait of the kind of father he will be.

Identifying the quality and nature of those three different types of relationships is one part of the assessment of a man's potential as a father. The other half of the assessment is a Field Test. It will only take a few hours, but it will reveal much, and the results are basically undeniable.

The Field Test is the Thanksgiving Day Test. It does not necessarily have to be administered on Thanksgiving to give a good result, but that date helps. Any large gathering of adults and children will provide the environment in which to conduct this experiment. But I recommend Thanksgiving because you can hide your true intentions and get a better and more accurate reading of your man and his potential to be a father.

Being a good father requires many things but first among them is a loving heart and the capacity for empathy and patience. The man who will be a good father has to bring himself down to the level of the child, not expect the child to come up to the level of the man. The man thus must be *childlike* so he can understand the point of view of the child he will try to father. For most men, in that they are 14 years old anyway and just pretending to be men, this should not be such a difficult challenge. But it often is. And thus comes the reveal you are looking for.

Here's the test. Bring your subject Man, possibly the father of your children someday, to a Thanksgiving Dinner. But not just any Thanksgiving Dinner. Bring him to one where there will be *lots of children* attending. In fact, the more children the better. And once in the house with all those little ones, just keep your eyes open and see what your man is up to and how he reacts. You are looking for the sympathetic vibrations that he will be feeling surrounded by all the kids. You are looking for the child in him to emerge and reveal itself. You are looking for him to either welcome the kids wholeheartedly or reject them wholesale. He will likely do one or the other. And that's what the test is designed to show you.

If he sees children running around all over the place, laughing and chasing each other, he will react one way or another. If his first reaction is to lean over to you and say, "Where are the parents of these monsters?" Then, you have just learned a lot and possibly all you need to know. The test may be over and done with. This particular man might not be ready yet. Same result if, when he hears them squealing and screaming, he rolls his eyes and drags you over to the bar for a double martini because the noise is already too much. That man might never be ready to be a dad. Just like a bunch of dudes do, a bunch of kids make a tremendous racket!

Alternatively, if he sees the children running and laughing and chasing each other and excuses himself so he can ask the host if he can sit at the kid's table for a little while, then this man has some real potential. You may have just learned all you need to know. This is a man who wants to be with the kids and is willing to put it out there like he is already truly one of them. This is a man who is completely in touch with the little boy inside him and he knows it. This is the man who has a chance to be a great father someday.

It's somewhat instinctual to be a good dad, but it's not a given that every man has that instinct at hand. And it's not that he will never be a good dad, it just means that he may not have found the rudder that can steer him and his child worthy craft through those particular waters, not yet anyway. He might only need a little training in the art.

One of my neighbors should be a dad some-day. He would probably end up in the Dad's Hall of Fame. Whenever we see him, he squats down to my son's level and they chat for a few minutes. Or when we've gone to his house, he takes my son by the hand and shows him all over the place and shares all his cool toys. Not because he wants to, he does this because he *has to*, his instinct has taken over and it's guiding him. He's practically on autopilot. He will be great at it, no doubt about it. Meanwhile, I have another neighbor. Unkind to his wife, impatient with his kids. Never asks a question he doesn't know the answer to and never answers a question without asking another question. Impatient, unforgiving, sad. His kids are trying always trying to please him but he never notices. His mother tolerated him. His wife probably wishes she had made other choices. His kids can't wait for me to visit. He is not an amaz-ing dad and the facts are there for all to see.

Men are asked to play many roles in their life-times, and the emphasis here is on the word 'play.' Whether husband, father, boyfriend, coach, role model, boss, whatever, it's simply a part we've been given to play. We have no idea how to actually 'be' any of these, at least not until we get in there and see what happens when we try. But like we have always done and will always do, we assume command, stink with confidence, bark out a few orders, and hope everyone sees how well we are doing.

We cannot help but reveal our instincts and our nature. They show up in everything we do, say, dream, dash, fulfill or falter. Especially when it comes to the most important role we will ever play: father.

So You Found Someone
New, Now What?

It's not easy to fall in love. Nor is it easy to stay in love. Even though it happens all the time, it's still a mystery and a miracle, wrapped in a quandary and a conundrum. But suppose it's happened to you. Suppose some surprise romance has sprung up out of nowhere and left you more hopeful than you've ever been before in your life. More thoughtful of your future and where it might be taking you. More capable of understanding that if you handle it right, you can affect the process that is sweeping your heart away.

Falling in love with someone is like finding a hummingbird has taken to building a nest in a little tree right near your window and all you want to do is let it happen and do nothing that will disturb it from happening. And all you want to see is what will happen next.

I was in such a moment. And more than anything else I wanted it to work and become one of the great loves of my life. Which it became and has remained. But it was not completely by accident. It was not *just* luck. I did everything in my power to make sure that the love affair that was beginning would never need to have an ending. And I came up with three rules.

Of all the discoveries I have made in my life, these three rules are the ones that I treasure most. Not only because they work but because they last. Not just for me but for anyone, man or woman – boy or girl, who finds themselves in that situation. The rules work and will work again and again. They allow a love affair to begin and find its footing. They allow two people to discover each other's wishes and hopes and possibilities, without prying or demanding anything. Ultimately, they will allow a love affair to become a love affair, and then, to thrive as a love affair. *If* that was what was meant to be.

My co-writer (the 14-year-old who's running and possibly ruining my life) keeps nudging me to go big or go home and write down an analogy he just thought of, so here it is: These rules are the Theory of Relativity, for couples.

Men and women fall in love all the time obviously, but do any of us really understand just how and why? For men it starts with the face and grows from there, like Spanish Moss. For women, who knows? As a child who drives and shaves, I honestly have no idea. It could be the time of day, the presence of alcohol, an absolutely perfect sunset, someone who makes you laugh maybe?

But whatever it is, what makes us fall in love with each other is a phenomenon that can be encouraged, massaged and even manipulated a little bit.

According to my research (again, this is a weak area for me, so let's just go with "instinct and intuition"), *we fall in love with each other completely by accident.* By complete chance. By a mixture of fate and random circumstance, which brings together two souls and lets them find in each other a perfect match, and ultimately, hopefully, a perfect mate. Good luck mixes with good timing and presents the opportunity of a lifetime. And if that happens, and you have a chance to be part of a great love affair, you must do everything possible to let it happen, keep it happening, and never ever get in its way.

I came up with these right after I met the lady in the rain, the amazing woman who would become my second wife. Right after she stopped by my office to say thank you for rescuing her. You just read about her a few pages ago. I knew that day in my office, almost immediately, that I *wanted* to be in love with her. She had cleaned up very nicely compared to the person I had met on the side of the road. In fact, she had one of the most beautiful faces I had ever seen, and she was smart as a whip, and well-mannered, and I could hear the 14-year-old inside me scream-ing that I better not screw this up.

I also knew that I wanted her to be in love with me, despite all the bridges we would have to cross to get there. Such as, that I was older, a different race, in the midst of a career, in the middle of a divorce, already had two young kids, and was traveling all over the world all the time. Obstacles? What obsta-cles? This is totally do-able, I remember thinking. After all, I have always been a big dreamer 14-year-old who sees anything as possible. Plenty of room under the tent for this remarkable woman and me to get together.

I dreamed up the rules over the next couple of days. They were a framework, a guide, a foundation that would allow the two of us to find each other's hearts without anything getting in the way. And if it was in the cards, to fall in love with each other. The rules would prevent either one of us from saying too much too soon or sharing more than was necessary under the circumstances. The rules would encour-age us to be ourselves, our truest selves, while being around someone new. The rules would keep us from ever making an unkind remark or a comment that would be hurtful and very possibly long-lasting. The rules would, most importantly, allow the relation-ship to be *all it could be*, especially at its very earliest and still very vulnerable stages. So, here's what I came up with to let all that happen.

RULE #1
Never Say Bad Things About Yourself

Whoever is falling in love with you doesn't need any impediments to that journey. So get out of the way and let it happen. Never say anything that would create a negative image about the person you've become. There is no need to share any of your undesirable traits and weaknesses. They are not who or what you are, just some lame habits you picked up along the way. Let the person who might fall in love with you someday paint their own portrait of you, without any suggestions, interference or negatives that diminish the possibility that you are amazing.

You are who you are, but some details are better lost than found.

If you mention, for instance, "My mother always thought I was a liar..." You will have planted the seed that you are, in fact, a liar. Or, at the very least, that you are probably a liar. Or, if you recall that your dad once called you a slut, that seed has now been planted and will grow like a dandelion on a hot summer day. Since the other person has no context and barely knows you at this early stage, you might as well get the word tattooed on your forehead.

It's like going to a new school. Tell just one person that your high cheekbones and black hair earned you the nickname "Tonto" at your old school, then that's it. You're Tonto at the new school too. Had you just kept that detail to yourself, you would not have any cruel monikers to worry about. So it's the same thing when you're at the start of a new love affair. Keep the bad things to yourself and you can just start over, fresh and clean, new.

This rule applies to everything and anything negative. If one eye is bigger than the other, or your nostrils flare when you laugh, or you think your hair is ratty, or that you look fat in a certain outfit, or whatever. Of course please mention your peanut allergy and deathly fear of rabbits. Good things to know! But skip the irritable bowel syndrome details. Or your hammer toe. Say something good or say nothing! Negatives comments about yourself are like graffiti: easy to spray on, very hard to clean off. Only share the things that will make the other person like you more!

RULE #2
Never Say Anything About Involuntaries

An involuntary is anything someone does without realizing they are doing that particular thing. And I think we fall in love with each other because of them, because of our involuntary actions and the responses those actions inspire. It's not the practiced motions or bits, the scripted words or worn out jokes we might tell, it is the accidental reveals that attract us to each other. It is the improvisational, extemporaneous, and unexpected things that someone does that really pulls the other person in deep and doesn't let them go.

So never acknowledge, compliment or in any other way discuss anything a person does that he or she *does not realize they are doing*. Their involuntaries in other words. These are the traits and mysteries that make each of us who we are, and different from everyone else, regardless of how insignificant a detail they may seem to be. The moment you tell someone about theirs, it ceases to be involuntary. From that moment on it will be a *voluntary* action, a determined act, and no longer a purely instinctive one.

I noticed on our first real date that my (soon to be) wife would hum a little song while she was eating. She was like a kid, listening to some tune that was playing in her head. I thought it was one of the sweetest things I had ever seen someone do, and I could hardly wait to see if she would do it again, and again. Which it turned out she did! I came to anticipate it and enjoy it all the more. She had no idea she was doing this of course, and if I had told her, she undoubtedly would have stopped it, or changed it, or done it too much, or something. So, I said nothing and never mentioned it. Even to this day. I made the conscious decision to let her be her.

She had other beautiful involuntaries too. When I would reach for her arm when we were walking together, she would move it away from her body to leave more room for my hand to get in there. When we were listening to music and standing in the back of a club, sometimes she would lean against me like I was a post. If she didn't hear what I said, she would cock her head to one side and raise an eyebrow, like a puppy, and ask me to repeat it. I loved all these little things she did, all her little instinctive involuntary actions, and never wanted any of them to change. I knew they were making me love and like her more and more, so I said nothing about them. Why tell her I noticed? She would have just become self-conscious about them and then they would soon stop. Ultimately, she would have become less her true self and less herself around me.

The beauty of this rule is that it allows human nature to serve us in one of the ways it was intended to serve us best. It allows us to be who we are around someone new without becoming too self-aware and restricting of our instincts and humanity. If you say anything about someone's involuntary actions, it's like a judgment. Yes a positive one, but nonetheless a judgment. And the involuntary thing will not survive it. A great example is someone's laugh. It takes a lifetime to find one. The moment you tell someone just how much you like their laugh, it changes it, forever. That person will never have that laugh again because they will have become self-conscious about it.

With anyone you're starting a love affair with, let them be who they are, and let them be themselves around you. And vicey versa. Deflect or dodge any compliments for your involuntaries. If someone says, "You know what you do that I love…?" Instead of saying, "What?" say instead, "Please don't tell me and maybe I'll do it again." Don't let someone compliment your giggle or the way you hum during dinner, or the way you brush a wall with your fingertips when you walk out of a room. Let your involuntaries remain forever involuntary.

RULE #3
If You Get Upset, Just Whisper

When a man meets a woman for the first time, his imagination is on High, and his heart is on Ready, and the longer she can keep him in that state of mind the greater the chance that he will fall in love with her, completely and forever. At early points in a relationship, if it's working, a man sees a face and thinks of nothing but beauty and love and happiness. That woman says his name and he gets a spray of dopamine that drenches his frontal lobes and makes him think he could live like that forever. A touch of a finger on a hand gets a tingle going down his spine. It's all happening as it should be happening. Nature is running its course.

But there is one thing that can bring the whole wonderful parade to a complete and grinding halt. Anger. Expressed anger. An angry voice can ruin everything and can easily destroy all the new love that was being built. Instantly. Like the rain washes away a chalked sidewalk portrait. It is upsetting and unsettling and makes the person on the receiving end feel diminished and thoroughly unimportant. You cannot take back something awful you said, no matter how many times you apologize, especially if you used an angry voice to say it.

If you say something critical, metallic, unloving, thoughtless... it will make the person you are speaking to/yelling at think that you are all those things, and that he or she was wrong to think you were something else. When you met, both of you thought of possibilities and promises, innocence and hope, and maybe even "could we fall in love with each other?" But the moment you tear into that person, it pierces the balloon like a pin does and ends the fantasy right there.

So, what happens if a man, for instance, does something legitimately idiotic? Let's say he shows up late or dresses inappropriately, forgets someone's name or loses the tickets to the movies again. You have to say something, right? You still get to share your feelings, right? Yes, yes, yes...

You do you have the right to make a comment. Or a suggestion. Or cast an aspersion if you must. But... *Just say it in a whisper.* Unless he's deaf, he will lean in to hear you better. He will not be as defensive. He will not mimic your attack and attack you right back. He will get all the words you say but without the searing sarcasm and biting vitriol. He will get the message without getting his heart broken. The whole situation could be discussed and resolved in 30 seconds, if you whisper the complaint and he whispers his apology right back, which he will by the way. (Us boys don't like being in trouble.

We will try to get out of it and back to something fun as soon as possible. Try it and see.)

My wife and I were at dinner with some friends a few weeks ago and we mentioned that we never argue. And that in all the years together we have never even had even an angry discussion. 21 years and counting... Our friends were astonished. When they asked how we did it, I told them about this rule. And the sweetest thing happened. Everyone started whispering at each other! And weeping as they did. (It gets very emotional when everyone is whispering important things they have to say!) But it was what was being said that was so amazing. R told C that he hated it when she raised her voice to him, and that it hurt his feelings. And he begged her, while whispering at her, to not do it again. She whispered back that she was sorry and that she had never known and agreed to try it. The other couple had me repeat how we did it, and they made a similar pact. So this rule is not just for beginners. Both these couples had been together for many years, and the angry voice was a hidden conflict that had never been resolved. Until that night anyway...

So those are the rules. Three rules for falling in love and staying in love, and letting people be themselves around you. Now, do these three rules actually work? Well, I live by them all, in most every situation and every friendship. I have never told my wife about her involuntary actions that I love, and I don't tell my sons or my friends about theirs either. I like it when people feel free to be just who they are around me. It's better for everyone that way. At the same time, I never volunteer anything bad about myself, just in case people might think less of me and run off to find better, newer friends. And an angry voice has no place in my life or my heart and I have not said anything with a mean voice in literally decades. My wife and I disagree rarely and always find a way to whisper ourselves out of it. So yes, in another answer to my own question, the rules do work and they will work. Just give them a chance.

Actually, Men *Can* Handle the Truth

Men aim to please. We love to please. We live to please. Sometime long ago, very early on in our development we realized that things got a lot sweeter in our lives if our partners were happy. The food got better, the bed got warmer, the cave (or house) was a much nicer place to be... All this but only if the person we were canoodling with was *also* happy. So, whether it's part of our dna or our collective wisdom, or a survival instinct, men have figured out that if we do more of what our partners want, and less of what we want, as long as it is within shouting distance of reasonable, things seem to get that much closer to perfect for us.

The flip side of this is that the partner has to be really clear about what it is they want and what it is that would make them happy. Nuances are for interpretive dancers. Suggestions are for librarians. Men want and need to know exactly and precisely what is expected of them. Down to the last detail. Leaving nothing to interpretation. Just come out and say it, whatever it is. I promise you we can handle it! Yes we can! Say it slowly and clearly and try to avoid big words. (Sounds exactly like a fourteen-year-old boy wrote this, doesn't it?)

This is all the truer when it comes to our love lives. Because we have no idea why the women in our lives love us. None whatsoever. We can hardly believe it when it happens. When someone falls in love with one of us, we feel the same as we would feel finding a lost winning lottery ticket. Whooo-Hoooo!! Look at any wedding album. More than likely the face on the groom displays childlike wonder and absolute disbelief that things turned out this way. He's shocked, but not in a bad way. He can hardly believe it himself. The little boy inside him pulled all the man levers correctly and now some remarkable woman is committing to a life to him. Wheeeeee!

My friend Danny has been married forever and will stay that way. He listens to his wife and she speaks to him in clear brief sentences. As a for instance, when they were just getting together, she saw that he had an interest in golf. She told him that her mother was a golf widow, and that her father was away almost all day, both Saturdays and Sundays, pursuing the fleeting perfection of a low handicap. For that reason she asked Danny not to play golf. So, you know what he did? He said okay. Never became a golfer. Despite how valuable it might have been for his career and socializing calendar, he responded to her request because she made it so clear. She didn't mess around with hints and allegations, suggestions and inference, she just came right out and said it: Please No Golf. And he listened. And it worked out great for everyone as a result. He gave up one little thing in exchange for a lifetime of her happiness. A simple sacrifice was made in response to a precise request. That's exactly how it should be. Danny and his wife found life partners in each other as a result of the way they communicate. She tells him what she wants, and he listens. His career was not impacted in the slightest as he went on to become one of the legends of his industry.

Theirs is a template that will work in almost any love affair. One person speaks from the heart, the other person listens. One could possibly make the argument that men don't listen unless they have to, or it's too late, but I would counter that men are better than that. Simpler than that. Easier to operate than that. The message just has to be straightforward and presented in a way that is uncomplicated and direct. It's like talking to a puppy. Tell him to sit, and he'll sit. Tell him to eat and he'll eat. Short sentences work perfectly well, and much better than long ones infused with emotion, history, far-flung departures and unnecessary details.

So much time is wasted trying to phrase things correctly, beating around the proverbial bush, finding nicer ways to say things instead of just plain truth. So unnecessary. Keep it simple. We'll get the message much better. Just tell us. Straight up. Whatever it is. We really do want to know. Especially when it comes to your heart and its tender mercies. Let us know what it is that would make you happy. Tell us how you want the story to unfold, and around that dream we can build a plan together to help you get there.

My wife and I were still in our first year of dating, and really still getting to know each other. By that time she had met my two remarkable sons from my first marriage and had fallen in love with both of them. So, she opened her heart to me one night and said, "I would love to have kids of my own – if that's what you would want." I was still married, still getting a divorce, still blazing along with my career, still making every effort to be a great dad, and still it was the easiest decision of the decade. I called her back the next day and said, "I must love you so much already. My answer is yes, let's do it." And we immediately began the process of having our own little guy. She made her wishes so clear and so easy to understand. There was little innuendo or room for doubt. There it was right in front of me. She wanted something and was unafraid to just say it. Luckily,

I was unafraid to hear it, and more than willing to act on it. Had she not been so honest with me, and so clear with what would make her happy, tragedy awaited us. It was while we were trying to get pregnant, with her taking supplements and vitamins and some bitter Chinese teas every day, that a terrible sickness was revealed. The ovarian cancer that was hiding inside her like an assassin responded to all the encouragement by unleashing itself and bursting to life! We were able to catch it in time and withdraw a few eggs before it was too late. Surgeries and chemo soon followed and our son spent five years as a zygote in a freezer in Torrance waiting for her to get better. Which she did, thankfully thankfully thankfully.

I cannot begin to imagine my life without the two of them in it.

All this to say that men can handle the truth. Be unafraid and just tell us what it is.

Epilog

A Final Thought Before I Go Back to My Fort

As has been mentioned here more than a few times, men are not all *that* complicated. We take direction well and it is easy to understand most, if not all, of our motivations. We are, generally speaking, easy to read, easy to understand, and easy to be with. We are, generally speaking, loyal and faithful, trustworthy and reliable. We are, generally speaking, very bad liars, despite all our practice at it. Only a small percentage of us are evil, although all of us are capable of it. We can, generally speaking, get along with almost anyone, provided that we are never criticized for anything we do or have ever done. We are portraits of grace and humility, generally speaking, provided that we are never asked to change anything about ourselves. We are a little selfish, but not as a lifestyle. If this all seems simple, it is.

Fourteen is the magic number here. Approach us like we are fourteen, interact with us like we are fourteen, be nice to us as if we are fourteen, and everything will work out just fine. Keep in mind that we are mature for our age and imagine that locked inside each one of us is a little boy operating a man robot. That's who we are and what we are. We pretend to be men and hope that none of the women in our lives ever figure that out.

Inside every man is a fourteen-year-old boy wondering what the hell happened. Everything was fine and then we got fat and hairy. But every man sticks to his plan nonetheless: Confidence before anything else. It has served him perfectly up until now, and more than likely will be the port in any storm he faces. But inside he is still a little confused, still somewhat mystified, still surprised at most of the things that have happened to him. Help him figure it out, or be eternally disappointed in his immaturity. It's up to you. Completely.

Men are uncomplicated. Easy to understand. Fun to partner with. Loyal like wolves. Dedicated to their families. Capable of great love.

But be thoughtful. Be kind. Don't try to improve us. Just tell us what we need to do better in clear and simple language. Try to tell us exactly what you want. The results will be remarkable. Most, if not all of the time, we will be faithful to you, respectful of your big dreams, and honored to be your partner in achieving life's greatest possibilities. Most of us boys are like that anyway. Ready and willing to love the ones who loves us back.

Acknowledgements

Thanks to all of these friends for their patient counsel and many suggestions.

Bob Davis
Portia Cohen
Susan Raihofer
Nicole Tibbetts
Karen Sturges
Jeff Eick
Karen Rehm
Karen Brenna
Cory Bergen
Luciana Moore
Kristin Maglonzo
Jenny Rosen
Scott Tobis
Janet Allen
Catherine Wyler
Tom DeCercio
Roxanne Arkie, RN
Dr. Kim Phinney
Jeff Adams

About the Author

Tom Sturges is an accomplished speaker, author, executive, mentor, father, and golfer.

He has published five books thus far, including the Amazon bestseller *Parking Lot Rules and 75 Other Ideas for Raising Amazing Children*. His other books are *Grow the Tree You Got, Every Idea a Good Idea, A Good Divorce Begins Here*, and *Preston Sturges: The Last Years of Hollywood's First Writer/Director*.

Tom has received fifty-plus commendations and awards from various mayors, governors, members of the House of Representatives, and senators for his work with at-risk, inner-city children via his foundation Witness to a Dream. A total of 233 kids benefited directly from his efforts and graduated high school to attend four-year colleges.

Tom spent thirty-five years as a talent finder in the music business and signed a number of important artists to publishing deals, including Red Hot Chili Peppers, Outkast and Goodie Mob, Smashing Pumpkins, Stone Temple Pilots, Foo Fighters, 50 Cent, Jack Johnson, and 3 Doors Down.

Tom is also a playwright and screenwriter.

www.ingramcontent.com/pod-product-compliance
Lightning Source LLC
Chambersburg PA
CBHW060135130626
46556CB00006B/2349